THE
NEW RULES
OF COLLEGE
ADMISSIONS

TEN FORMER ADMISSIONS OFFICERS
REVEAL WHAT IT TAKES
TO GET INTO COLLEGE TODAY

STEPHEN KRAMER
MICHAEL LONDON
FOUNDERS, COLLEGE COACH

A FIRESIDE BOOK
PUBLISHED BY SIMON & SCHUSTER
New York   London   Toronto   Sydney

FIRESIDE
Rockefeller Center
1230 Avenue of the Americas
New York, NY 10020

FIRESIDE and colophon are registered trademarks
of Simon & Schuster, Inc.

For information regarding special discounts for bulk purchases,
please contact Simon & Schuster Special Sales at 1-800-456-6798 or
business@simonandschuster.com.

Designed by Jan Pisciotta

Manufactured in the United States of America

10   9   8   7   6   5   4   3   2   1

Library of Congress Cataloging-in-Publication Data
Kramer, Stephen.
    The new rules of college admissions : ten former admissions officers
reveal what it takes to get into college today / Stephan Kramer, Michael
London.
       p.   cm.
"A Fireside book."
Includes index.
    1. Universities and colleges—United States—Admission—Handbooks,
manuals, etc. 2. College applications—United States—Handbooks,
manuals, etc. I. London, Michael. II. Title.
LB2351.2.K73 2006   378.1'610973—dc22   2006944342

ISBN-13:   978-0-7432-8067-9
ISBN-10:   0-7432-8067-9

In memory of
Mark London

Contents

CONTENTS

Introduction

The spark for College Coach began when we were in high school more than twenty years ago.

We both wondered how the college process could be so fascinating and yet so frightening. Why couldn't our high school tell us what to do? Even our parents admitted they didn't know how to guide us. (And we have very smart parents.)

Today, the college admissions process is even more challenging and makes people even more uncomfortable. Parents and students are now faced with an ultracompetitive process and more decisions than ever. Although a lot of helpful information about college admissions exists on the Web, families are teased into believing that they can find a solution in cyberspace. To make matters worse, many of the tactics that were effective years ago are no longer valid.

The rules of college admissions have changed.

As the founders of College Coach, the largest educational consulting firm in America, our mission is to maximize each student's chances of success. We have consulted to families across the country and all over the world. In addition, corporations regularly sponsor our efforts for employees and their families.

Based upon our experience counseling thousands of families, we find that the best person to assist a student through the college process is the parent, which is why much of our writing in this book is geared to you, the mother or father. Parents want to do everything they can to help their children succeed, and this book offers a one-stop resource to ensure your child makes a successful transition from high school to college.

This book makes three promises to you:

- We will show you how the rules of college admissions have changed over the years and how your child can come out ahead in today's admissions environment. There are now more colleges, more test prep programs, and more application-savvy students. As you will learn, colleges that used to be considered safety schools ten or twenty years ago are now much more competitive.

- We will show you how your child can be accepted to the school that is right for his needs and that he is excited to attend. There are many, many schools out there, and we will help narrow your child's application list and apply the very best strategy for gaining acceptance.

- Finally, the college admissions process doesn't have to be stressful. We demystify the application process by offering numerous expert tips on preplanning, scheduling, organizing, and communicating to help you and your family achieve results and minimize conflict. After all, what's the point of helping your child get into college if you end up driving each other crazy in the process?

Whether you are immersed in the application process already or you are the parent of a high school freshman, this book will help you to help your child. *The New Rules of College Admissions* is a comprehensive, step-by-step guide on how to select, apply to, and finance college. Our goal is to save your family time, money, and anxiety.

Each chapter is written by a seasoned expert from College Coach. Our team of consultants, led by Lloyd Peterson, vice president of education, are all former senior admissions officers. They have worked at the top colleges in the country, including Yale, Columbia, Northwestern, the University of Pennsylvania, and others. Reading this book is like having an admissions insider advising you every step of the way. Each chapter provides critical information about a single piece of the application process—from crafting a personal essay, deciding which tests to take and when, creating a college list, securing helpful letters of recommendation, and acing the interviews.

Throughout the book you will come across helpful sidebars entitled "Don't Panic!" "Warning!" and "New Rules of College Admissions." "Don't Panic" sidebars address some of parents' most common fears and offer tactics for making the best of admissions challenges. "Warning!" sidebars clue you in to some of admissions officers' pet peeves and offer vital information on actions that can hurt your child's chances of getting in. And "New Rules of College Admissions" highlight concepts that may be quite different from parents' own experiences with the college admissions process. Paying particular attention to the information in each of these sidebars can give your child a significant edge.

You will also find plenty of additional exercises, dos and don'ts, case studies, and checklists to guide you. Ultimately, the goal of this book, like the goal of College Coach, is to simplify the college admissions process and help your child attend the school that's the best fit for all of his needs.

More than 80 percent of the students College Coach assists get into their top-choice college. And like your child, these students come from families with the highest of expectations. We are proud of our track record and look forward to making your child's process a successful one, too.

Take a deep breath and start reading—you are just a few hundred pages away from being able to smoothly guide your child through a most difficult and complex process.

We look forward to working with you and wish you the best of luck!

Stephen Kramer and Michael London
Founders, College Coach

CHAPTER 1

THE HIGH SCHOOL EXPERIENCE

**Expert Coach: Karen Crowley,
Former Admissions Officer, University of Pennsylvania**

What is the one thing virtually every college applicant has in common?

High school.

Every student is different, but the experience of ninth through twelfth grade is the common denominator among all college applications. The good news is that this portion of the college application process is familiar to you already. You have guided your child through school since kindergarten, so you no doubt have plenty of experience helping your child make decisions about which classes and activities he should sign up for. Now it's time to approach those same types of decisions from the perspective of a college admissions officer.

What are college admissions officers looking for when it comes to a student's high school experience? They want to see a young adult with some understanding of what he's good at, how he applies himself, what he is dedicated to, and how others perceive him. To determine these answers, they assess academics, extracurricular activities, and a student's reputation. In this chapter I will share specific success strategies to help you and your child make the best choices in each of these three areas.

RULES TO REMEMBER IN THIS CHAPTER

- **Report cards matter most.** Academics are *the* most important factor to admissions officers. Pay close attention to your child's course selection and grades through every year of high school.
- **Colleges like students with passion and commitment.** The best applicants demonstrate unique extracurricular pursuits that involve leadership, personal growth, and genuine enjoyment and enthusiasm.
- **Reputation counts.** Colleges seek out the opinions of teachers and administrators when assessing a student. Having a reputation as a good school citizen can tip the scales in favor of your child's application.

I. ACADEMICS

Make no mistake about it: academics are the most important factor to admissions officers when making a final admissions decision.
Despite all the tips and strategies you're likely to hear about essays, interviews, teacher recommendations, and other parts of the college application, academics are, bar none, the most important piece of a student's profile. If admissions officers believe that an applicant cannot meet the academic challenge at a particular college, that child will not be admitted. After all, we are talking about a student at one school applying to become a student at another school. All other aspects of the application process are certainly important, but none influences the yes or no decision as much as the admissions officer's complete academic analysis. The components of that analysis, which will be explored in detail in this chapter, include:

- **Academic Picture.** What is the "at-a-glance" view of the student's academic track record? What are the exact, "unweighted" grades (number of As, Bs, Cs, et cetera) each year? What level of courses (honors, advanced placement, et cetera) has the student taken? What curriculum choices has the student made? What is the yearly GPA (grade point average) and the combined GPA of freshman, sophomore, and junior years?

- **Context.** In looking at a student's transcript, what courses does the particular high school offer and how did this student fare within the given academic environment? Also, are there any extenuating circumstances in the student's life to consider—such as a divorce, death of a family member, or a learning disability—that may have affected academic performance?

- **Profile.** When the admissions officer evaluates the above factors, what is the overall impression of the student? For instance, "This is a smart, ambitious scientist who struggles with English composition," or "This is a girl with great fluency in foreign languages who continues to plug away in increasingly difficult math classes even though it hurts her GPA," or "This is a boy who struggled his freshman year but really applied himself and improved his grades over time." The profile is a more complex— and forgiving—academic representation of a student than the straight numbers of a GPA.

The better you understand what admissions officers are looking for in your child's high school academic record, the better you can help your child make decisions about what courses to take, what grades to strive for, and what trade-offs might be beneficial.

Academic Course Selection

It is essential to become familiar with the academic options at your child's school as soon as possible. Conscientious course selection is vital preparation for the college admissions process. Using the strategies below, you should review the course catalogue with your child before each school year to help plan what classes he would like to take and how that fits into his college— and life—aspirations. It is never too early to be planning for each year's slate of classes, so get a copy of the course catalogue as soon as possible. If your child is in ninth or tenth grade, you can follow all of the guidelines below. If your child is in eleventh or twelfth grade, don't agonize about choices your child has already made, but do your best to help maximize remaining course selections. Helping choose the best courses each semester requires an ongoing conversation with your child, one that may develop and change dramatically throughout high school. Your overall goal should be to have a child who is happy, challenged, and achieving the best grades possible. To help guide you, here are my answers to parents' most frequently asked questions about course selection and, its soul mate, GPA:

Q: What courses are absolutely essential year by year?

A: Every college-bound student must enroll in each of the five "academic solids," for at least the first two years of high school. The five solids are:

- **English.** English is English. You've got to have it.
- **Social Science History.** This is also a classic standard.
- **Mathematics.** Almost any college degree will require math, so colleges are more comfortable with kids who will make it easily through college math courses. Four years of math is highly recommended. Note that "traditional" math is preferred over specialized math, so encourage your child to take geometry rather than business math.
- **Science, preferably with lab.** Lab science requires critical thought, which colleges believe is needed. Three to four years of science is preferable, and biology, chemistry, and physics are preferred. Of course, your daughter should not drop science if she is planning to be premed!
- **Foreign Language.** Foreign language courses with literature study are recommended over conversation when there is an option.

Most colleges prefer to see a student enroll in all five academic solids each year of high school. At the least, they favor students with four years of English and math and three years of a foreign language and science. Eleventh and twelfth graders have the most leeway when it comes to taking all five academic solids. After careful consideration and consultation with an academic adviser or guidance counselor, upperclassmen may choose to drop an academic solid in favor of another class related to personal interests or future goals. For instance, a boy with a flair for creative writing and a summer internship to study poetry in Europe may opt to take an additional foreign language course in lieu of AP physics during his senior year. A girl who is planning to go into engineering may drop Spanish class after junior year in order to take an additional math class or science lab.

Q: **How do colleges compare GPAs from school to school when students take various course loads and different schools have different grading systems?**

A: What you see on your child's high school transcript is not necessarily how colleges will see that transcript. Colleges use their own proprietary weighting system for high school grades. These probably do not coincide with your high school's system.

The most common way colleges approach this is by recalculating a student's GPA from ninth to eleventh grade based solely on his five academic solids. Most schools use a three-year cumulative average and then let the senior year stand alone as a final factor.

To compare students regardless of grading systems, admissions officers will most likely recalculate the five core subjects using a four-point, unweighted scale. In such a scale, an A = 4, a B = 3, and so on. (An "unweighted" GPA is calculated based on the actual grade in each class, regardless of the level of the class. A "weighted" GPA takes into consideration both the class level and the student's grade.)

Here is a chart to help you calculate your child's unweighted GPA.

Subject	Grade 9 Final Grade (scale of 0-4)	Grade 10 Final Grade	Grade 11 Final Grade	Average
English				
Math				
Science				
Social Science				
Foreign Language				
			"Unweighted" Core Subject GPA =	

What happens after an admissions officer calculates an unweighted GPA? He then goes course by course and gives his own weighting to the courses based on the difficulty level of each. Sometimes this is done in his head and sometimes in writing based on a college's very specific point system. Unfortunately, there is no way to know how each school approaches this process, but it's important to know that they do not take your child's high school transcript at face value.

Q: Is it better for my child to take easier courses and get As, or take harder courses (such as AP classes) and get Bs?

A: The answer to this question greatly depends on the college or university in question.

As a general rule, admissions officers look favorably upon the student who challenges himself academically rather than take an easy A. When it comes to helping your child decide which courses to take and at what level of difficulty, realistically assess what each course will add to the student's overall transcript and application in light of the level of schools he wants to attend.

If your child is applying to Yale, Harvard, Stanford, or other highly selective schools, you probably won't be surprised to learn that your child has to take AP classes *and* get As. At these schools, most candidates will have achieved stellar grades in the most challenging classes.

On the other hand, schools admitting greater than 50 percent of their applicants, such as Indiana University, the University of Pittsburgh, and the University of Arizona, are likely to accept a weaker course load, but they still look for a consistent record of hard work, achievement, and improvement of grades over time.

Of course, a wide range of schools occupy the middle ground. Here is a basic chart to help you understand what course levels and grades are most common at a variety of schools. This is not a comprehensive list, but it will give you an idea of where your child sits in the spectrum and what grades are needed to be seriously considered by various schools.

Competitiveness of School	Examples of Schools in this Category	Course Levels of Most Applicants	Grades Achieved in Courses
Premier	Harvard, Yale, Princeton, Dartmouth, Stanford	AP and honors whenever available	As
Top	Cornell, Duke, Georgetown, Amherst, Williams	AP and honors whenever available	A-s and As
Very Good	Emory, Washington University, Wellesley, NYU, Vanderbilt	Majority AP and honors	An occasional B is acceptable
Good	George Washington University, Boston University, Lehigh, Union College, University of Richmond	Some AP and honors	50/50 split between As and Bs

Above Average	University of Vermont, Temple, Indiana University, Northeastern, Baylor, University of Colorado at Boulder	AP and honors are less common	Bs are normal, and the occasional C
Average	University of Hartford, Hofstra, St. Johns, University of Tampa, Old Dominion	Almost no AP and honors	Cs are okay, but Bs are preferred

Challenge, rigor, and high hopes for college acceptance are important, but you must also be realistic when assessing your child's course selection and subsequent GPA. You don't want to set your child up for mediocre grades or even failure. If a student's grade in a particular course goes down an entire mark (say, from a B to a C, as opposed to a B to a B-), that's a signal that his course load is probably too difficult. It is always better to be a B student than a C student, regardless of curriculum. When in doubt, talk to your child's academic advisers when deciding what course levels your child should take.

Q: What elective courses look best to colleges? And do elective course grades matter?

A: Since school today is not just about the three Rs of reading, 'riting and 'rithmetic, your child also has elective courses to consider. What do college admissions officers look for when evaluating performance in these subjects? I like to think of electives as rounding out a student's picture. The selection of electives and the student's grades in those courses can help to reinforce the application's overall theme. For instance, if a girl is a theater junkie and writes her college essay on *CATS*, I would expect to see that she has theater, choir, or dance in her course load and she has performed well in these electives.

If your child is less focused and wants to experiment with electives and other nonacademic courses, there is nothing wrong with showing a genuine curiosity and trying a variety of classes, from computer science to studio art. Again, this helps tell a story. Perhaps your son is a Renaissance man who wants to combine his interests in science, music, and technology. No matter what the story, it's best to demonstrate good grades in elective courses. But keep in mind that the grades in these electives are not as important as the grades in the five core subjects. In other words, an A in art is nice, but don't expect your kid to get into MIT with an A in art and a B in chemistry. However—and this is a strong warning— poor grades in elective classes are a red flag to admissions officers. They imply a negative attitude and work ethic, and they can change an admissions officer's feelings about an applicant. Bad grades in gym class raise concerns that a kid with otherwise stellar grades is not really the all-around winner he appeared to be.

The High School Transcript

Have you ever seen your child's high school transcript—not the report card, but the official transcript? If you are like most parents, the answer is probably no. I am often surprised to learn that many families have never seen this important document, yet they eagerly instruct guidance counselors to send it directly to colleges! Often, families, and even the students themselves, don't know what the transcript looks like or what information appears on it.

It is important to request, study, and carefully proofread your child's high school transcript prior to sending it to an admissions office at any college or university. The more you know about your child's transcript, the better you will understand what admissions officers will see when getting to know your child and his high school. Here are some questions to answer about the transcript:

- Does the transcript show absences and tardies?
- Are state or national tests reported?
- Are final exam grades reported?
- Are every semester's grades reported or just final grades?

- Is there a grade distribution or class rank printed right on the transcript?
- How is the grade point average calculated?

Knowledge is power when it comes to the contents of your child's transcript. If you feel that the appearance of any of the above information could negatively impact your child's application, then you can do something about it sooner rather than later. For instance, a large number of absences and tardies can cause an admissions officer to question a child's motivation. If your son has a lot of absences his sophomore year, you may want to address the reasons for the absences elsewhere in the application, such as in a note from a guidance counselor or a mention in a teacher recommendation. If he was absent because of an illness like mono, colleges should know he wasn't just slacking off.

WARNING!

When it comes to any questionable aspect of your child's high school record—or any other problematic issue on his college applications—it's best to have a guidance counselor or teacher address it, rather than the parent or applicant. When parents and students try to make excuses for something negative on a child's application, admissions officers are pretty skeptical and rarely believe the complaint is unbiased. A third-party explanation is much more credible, so talk to your child's guidance counselor if you feel any information needs to be explained.

Also be aware that you might even find a factual error, either in a grade reported or even an actual class listed. This is another good reason to review your child's transcript before it gets into the hands of an admissions officer. If you do discover an error, report it to your school's guidance office and ask how to follow the procedure to fix it. If an actual grade is incorrect, be as relentless as you need to be to make sure the transcript is accurate. Some high schools do not like to make changes, but it is crucial that any inaccuracies are corrected before the transcript is distributed.

Why is it so important to have an accurate high school transcript? At a selective school, there is no single piece of the application that admissions officers spend more time with than the high school transcript. They read it, analyze it, and study it, which means that you should too. This is often the first document an admissions officer reviews, and it influences how she sees everything else in a student's file. I have found that many college applicants spend hours proofreading and agonizing over every other element of their application, yet have never studied the transcript to ensure that it is accurate. Don't make this mistake.

Admissions officers look at the transcript to assess a student's overall performance, grade level performance, individual subject performance, and to examine the rigor of a student's elected courses. These elements are each evaluated within the context of what a particular high school offers.

Let's go inside the mind of the admissions officer to learn how she is reading your child's transcript. By understanding the ways an admissions officer evaluates a transcript, you can perform the same critical assessment.

1. How did this student do compared to other kids at the same high school?

If older students from the same high school have applied to the college where your child is applying (which is usually the case), then it's a good bet that the admissions officers are familiar with your child's high school and will have some context with which to evaluate his performance. How do they remember all of the high schools across the country? Typically, colleges and universities keep records about the students they admit from a given high school, and admissions officers will be familiar with the academic profile a "competitive" student should maintain within a particular school. In other words, it is likely that the admissions officer will know, based on prior experience with your child's school, whether he is really a contender.

An admissions officer's personal experience and files are then confirmed by an official document called the High School Profile. Almost all high schools in the United States, and many throughout the world, produce this document on an annual basis and make it available to colleges. The High School Profile acts as a cheat sheet to help admissions officers quickly familiarize themselves with the high school and its classes. The profile will note many things, typically including, but not limited to:

information on community, setting, and faculty;
graduating class and school size;
comparative data on GPA distribution;
course options including level of difficulty and weight;
extracurricular opportunities;
postsecondary options for graduating seniors, including number attending
    college (listing most popular choices), number of seniors entering the
    military, number of seniors entering the work force.

It is critical to familiarize yourself with this public document so you can get the most objective picture of your child's achievements and choices within the context of your particular school. You can request a copy of the High School Profile from the guidance office. But remember that it is the school's job—not yours—to help college admissions offices best understand the school and the context in which students are performing.

If you are concerned about your school's profile document, or your child attends a nontraditional school such as a charter school that you fear may not be on the radar screen of colleges, set up an appointment with your child's guidance office to share your concerns. Guidance counselors will work with you to make sure colleges receive the information they need to assess your child's academic record.

WARNING!

Do not attempt to share your opinion about your child's High School Profile with a college admissions office. Writing a letter or calling an admissions office to say, "Earning a B average at my son Adam's school is like an A average at another school" will irritate busy admissions officers and will not do Adam any favors. Take time to review and understand the High School Profile, but that's all. Again, all concerns should be discussed with your high school guidance office rather than directly with the college.

2. What is the student's personal academic track record?

In other words, is this student's stock on the rise or the decline? In my experience, a weak freshman year is generally forgiven (it's the tail end of puberty, after all), while a poor junior or senior year isn't. Obviously admissions officers favor consistently strong students, but next best are students who steadily improved their performance and pursued increasingly tougher classes throughout high school. However, as discussed above, a challenging course load should not be undertaken at the expense of good grades.

NEW RULE OF COLLEGE ADMISSIONS: TWELFTH GRADE MATTERS—A LOT

Some of us may remember slacking off during our own senior years, but twelfth-grade performance has become increasingly important. This is because applicant pools have grown larger and more competitive. Strong grades during the first half of senior year are critical in supporting your child's college applications. Admissions officers at schools of all levels believe that senior year is a good predictor of college academic performance. Few admissions officers reach a conclusion regarding an early decision or early action candidate without these marks, and they almost always evaluate the first-half twelfth-grade marks before admitting a regular decision candidate.

3. How has this student performed in each subject area as a whole?

This part of the transcript review can be helpful for a student who has either a distinct weakness or a distinct strength. For example, a recent immigrant who has just learned English may look like a weak candidate based on overall GPA. However, after careful assessment, the admissions officer may note that weak English grades during freshman and sophomore year are pulling down the overall average. But as a potential engineering student, the candidate will take only limited college English courses. The admissions officer may ultimately favor the student for his highly impressive science and math grades in advanced courses. Furthermore, if the English grades are improving annually, this will help the candidate's case and boost the admissions officer's confidence in his future academic success. This admissions officer would read the remaining file for further evidence that the language skills are sufficient to do well at the school.

The reverse may be true for a native speaker who wants to study creative writing and foreign languages. Let's say this student elected to take two foreign languages throughout high school and earned excellent grades in both. He also performed well in the required and elective English classes. However, the math grades were consistently weaker. In this case, the admissions officer might look for an outstanding personal statement, combined with other evidence that supports a distinct talent and interest.

DON'T PANIC! WHAT IF MY CHILD'S GRADES ARE INCONSISTENT OR HAVE GONE DOWNHILL?

What can you do if your child does not have stellar grades across the board or has not improved over time? If this is the case in your family, here are four potential strategies:

1. If you believe your son really is a good student, but just hasn't "applied himself," you can think especially carefully about teachers who will help portray your child as a good student in a letter of recommendation.

2. If your daughter had poor grades in one subject but has positive academic attributes and a decent or better relationship with the teacher, you can ask that particular teacher to write a recommendation about your daughter's positive attitude, participation in class, tenacity, or desire to challenge herself.
3. Ask your child's guidance counselor to directly address the academic record in his letter and work on a story in which the academic record is portrayed in the context of other, more positive achievements.
4. Emphasize other achievements in the application, to the extent that they overshadow the poor grades. For example, demonstrate incredible achievement in an extracurricular activity through short-answer essays or the personal statement. This is not easy to pull off, but it is possible.

In all of the above strategies, make sure your student does not overtly attempt to "excuse away" poor grades in the personal statement or a separate letter. This almost always sounds like a whiny excuse to admissions officers and does not help your child's cause.

II. EXTRACURRICULARS

Analyze and then build upon your child's personal qualities and interests to create a powerful extracurricular profile.

It's rare for a student to be accepted to a highly selective college on brainpower alone. A strong extracurricular profile is also important. It aids students, parents, administrators, and college admissions officers alike in understanding a child as a whole person. Here are some specific benefits related to extracurricular activities:

• Students develop nonacademic skills, earn a sense of accomplishment, and meet peers and mentors outside of class. A student might forge a bond with faculty members, discover something he's good at, or learn how to handle responsibility. All of these benefits will also help during the college application process when it comes to letters of recommendation, essay topics, and interview discussions.

- Parents get assurance that their children are productive after school and learning life skills during their youth. Understanding your child's natural interests also helps you guide him through the college selection and application process.
- School administrators benefit from an involved and engaged student body. They are also better able to advise students on their future pursuits based on knowledge of their nonacademic interests.
- Admissions officers can forecast how the applicant may participate on campus to help make the college a more interesting place.

Students can also showcase certain strengths or interests with extracurricular activities. For example, a student might build upon an interest in writing by editing the school newspaper. A girl might demonstrate real scientific ingenuity with a powerful research project. A boy could showcase his athletic abilities through participation in junior varsity and varsity athletics. You will find multiple examples of various students' extracurricular profiles on the following pages. As you read through, keep in mind the concept of your child's "theme," which we will discuss in depth in chapter 5. The application theme is a clear and consistent description of a student that is demonstrated and reiterated through the application, including the extracurricular profile. The theme, which is unique to each child, helps focus the admissions officer on the key points about your child that will help him get accepted.

Each child's extracurricular profile is unique, but there are many tactics you can use to make sure your child's extracurricular story fits with his overall theme and helps build a strong college application. To begin, here is an overall, year-by-year guide to helping your child choose school-related extracurricular activities based on what a college admissions officer will be looking for.

	Year-by-Year Extracurricular Planning Guide
Grade 9	Explore a variety of interests, with the goal of selecting a few to pursue longer-term.
Grade 10	Build skills and experience in a few activities; take on increased responsibility (e.g., join committees or run for a higher student council position); build relationships with faculty leaders of clubs or coaches of sports teams for future recommendations.
Grade 11	Look for leadership opportunities in clubs, sports teams, music groups, et cetera. Seek out-of-school opportunities to expand on interests and pursue unique angles on skills (see "Using Your Community" section below).
Grade 12	Remain involved in activities and solidify leadership roles, relationships with adult leaders, and related out-of-school pursuits.

NEW RULE OF COLLEGE ADMISSIONS: THE MYTH OF THE WELL-ROUNDED APPLICANT

Being "well-rounded" is no longer a ticket to Harvard. While admissions officers are looking to create a well-rounded student body overall, they are less and less impressed by kids who are interested in many diverse areas. When all else is equal, a child with a deep interest and talent in one area will get in before a well-rounded candidate.

Don't get me wrong; well-roundedness isn't *bad*. If your child is an athlete, scholar, musician, and volunteer, then he will do well in the college admissions process. But if a child shows a discernible weakness—for example, he is a stellar athlete and musician who gets poor grades in several subjects—then his "well-roundedness" loses its luster. Well-rounded students need something extra to stand out, such as a strong leadership position or award in one area.

This is where extracurricular activities take on additional importance. If your daughter is strong in science and wants to be a veterinarian someday, then her application will be even stronger if she spends her summers working in a lab or volunteers at an animal shelter.

Using Your Community to Find Unique Activities

When most parents think about extracurriculars, they focus on activities offered by their child's high school. Think beyond that world. One of the best things you can do to help your child develop a unique extracurricular profile is to start thinking creatively and doing research to find activities outside of the school system to match your child's interests. Your community no doubt has hundreds of opportunities waiting to be discovered. One common technique career counselors use to help job seekers find networking opportunities is to create a list of every single person they know and the activities they are involved with. You can use this same technique when trying to find challenging after-school and summer experiences for your child.

The goal of pursuing activities outside of the school environment is to help your child challenge himself and go beyond the norm of high school-related extracurriculars. While thousands of kids' applications will include activities like football, student council, debate team, and other school-sponsored clubs, your child can stand out by doing something different. This is a particularly important tactic for students who may not have a successful track record in academics or school activities and need to compensate.

Opportunities are truly everywhere. When I think about my personal resources, I realize that I know a contractor who might offer a high school student summer work. I know a physician who might allow a student to work in his office. I know local business-people in real estate, catering, publishing, and computer systems who might welcome a young person in their workplaces. I know the president of the civic association, who may enjoy having a young person chair a committee or organize an event. There's also the local newspaper, radio station, library, humane society, soup kitchen, volunteer network, and halfway house—all places that often have interesting opportunities for high school students.

Summers are a great time to pursue non-classroom activities, especially if a student is involved with high school commitments during the year. Many families feel that expensive leadership, community service, or precollege programs are the most valuable, but there are many other, less expensive ways for students to have a meaningful, enjoyable summer experience that can also help their college applications. For students who need to make money over the summer, there are many paid opportunities as well.

For instance, I worked with a student, Emily, whose father volunteered at an assisted-living facility. The father noticed the evening social hour lacked spirit and suggested that Emily accompany him and bring her clarinet. She played music for an hour, much to the delight of the residents. Soon after, Emily placed an ad in the local newspaper and made announcements at her high school asking other musicians to participate in monthly concerts at the center. The seniors loved the music, Emily demonstrated her leadership skills, and to top it off, the total cost was limited to a newspaper ad.

What are some other out-of-school activities that have impressed me? I've admitted students who have rallied in political protests, designed and created their own clothes, or started their own businesses. While some activities require a great deal of initiative to get started, others take only a simple phone call to investigate established programs, yet all these pursuits are beneficial. A college admissions officer will consider a student to be an involved, creative self-starter when he sees the world beyond his high school.

WARNING!

While I cannot overemphasize the positive value of community activities to a student's extracurricular profile, your child should not completely disregard school-related programs. Colleges want to see students who take initiative outside of school, but they also want to accept students who will actively participate in the campus community. Be sure to encourage a balance.

Building a Strong Extracurricular Profile

What is the right balance of extracurricular activities for a student to present to a college? A strong extracurricular profile isn't easy to define but an admissions officer, she knows it when she sees it. Colleges look for sustained commitment, increased responsibility over time, creativity, a demonstration of the student's strengths, and a genuine enthusiasm for the activities that appear on the list. As discussed above, the best profiles involve both in-school and out-of-school activities and create the overall sense of a theme for the student.

Let's get more specific. When I talk about a demonstration of the student's strengths, I mean that the student is selecting activities in which he demonstrates some natural ability. Typically, this means that his activities mirror his academic strengths in some way, which contributes to a strong application theme. For instance, a student who loves to write and has good grades in English might read a lot, write for the school literary magazine, or spend a summer working at a library or bookstore. An excellent science student who is shy and not a natural leader might volunteer as a tutor for young children or run on the cross-country team rather than pursue a more team-oriented sport. Admissions officers understand that kids have a variety of personalities; they don't expect everyone to be football captain or first-chair violinist!

How do admissions officers gauge a student's genuine enthusiasm? They aren't mind readers, but they use common sense.

Enthusiasm is usually assumed when a student participates in a cluster of activities that seem to fit together, such as a lot of community service, school spirit activities, or political participation. Remember that your child will have more than one opportunity to demonstrate an interest in extracurricular pursuits. As you will learn in future chapters, extracurriculars are often a key component of college essays, short-answer questions, letters of recommendation, and interviews. Your child's enthusiasm for a particular pursuit or group of activities can shine through in these other areas. So, beyond helping your child choose which activities to pursue, it's also important to discuss what the activity means to him, since he will have to articulate this in these various components of the college application process. He should be able to articulate what he's learned from participating in each activity, what it has taught him about himself in his life now and related to his future goals, and whether or not he enjoyed the experience and why.

Here are several examples of successful extracurricular choices made by students, with an emphasis on the "profile" or "story" portrayed in each, and how each student's genuine interests and enthusiasm shined through:

Example 1: The Successfully "Themed" Well-Rounded Student

Dylan was a starter and captain of three varsity sports, even though he wasn't quite good enough to play any of them in college. Additionally, he volunteered to mentor a middle-school student, wrote columns for the school paper, and participated in meaningful social science research for four years. He has also participated in Model Congress and was active in his temple youth group during ninth and tenth grades.

The main themes I see in Dylan's diverse extracurricular profile are leadership and civic responsibility. He's a significant leader in his school community, has been selected as a role model in two venues (sports captain and volunteer mentor), and, even with a full high school course schedule, he participated in both in-school and out-of-school activities. To round out Dylan's profile, he listed his future ambition as a desire to study journalism and continue to hone his leadership and mentoring skills. In my mind, this all fits and makes Dylan an excellent candidate for admission, assuming his academic record is also strong.

DON'T PANIC! WHAT IF MY CHILD HAS NOT PARTICIPATED IN ANY— OR VERY FEW—ACTIVITIES?

Sometimes, although it is rare, an exceptional academic record will help to compensate for a lack of extracurricular activities, but not at the most selective schools, where admissions officers want the complete package. Kids really do need to be involved if they want to get into college. Even if this means that your child joins a club or starts volunteering at the beginning of his senior year, that is better than having no activities at all.

If you are already involved in the application process and it is too late for your child to add more extracurriculars to his profile, you will have to work extra hard to create an overall image that a college will look upon favorably. For instance, I know a young woman who has very good grades at a top public high school and strong test scores. However, she has participated in only one or two activities throughout high school. While her lack of activities meant that she could not apply to the highest-tier colleges in the country, she found ways to improve her chances at very good schools. For instance, she included hobbies, travel, and family activities on her application activities list. She also worked very hard to create stellar essays that reflect her spunk and personality, and used her essays to say that she has learned she could be a more complete person by stretching herself to be involved in pursuits outside her comfort zone. Part of her theme is to convince colleges that she is eager to be more involved on campus than she has been in high school.

Example 2: The Committed Leader

Lily attended an international high school and served as a student council representative in ninth and tenth grades, treasurer in eleventh grade, and class president in twelfth. She was a junior reporter in ninth grade, features editor in tenth and eleventh grades, and then coeditor in chief of the school newspaper senior year. She was also a four-year member of the basketball team, an avid photographer, and a devoted community servant (her family runs an annual benefit for a homeless shelter).

Like Dylan, Lily had a depth of commitment that shone through, with four years of involvement in each pursuit and a steady path of increasing responsibility and leadership. When evaluating Lily's overall profile it was clear that she was a natural leader who was committed to contributing as deeply as possible to each of her pursuits. Was she captain of the basketball team? No, but she stuck with it for four years. Did she win any awards for her photography? No, but she pursued a passion and also remained interested in it even with other time-consuming activities on her plate.

DON'T PANIC! WHAT IF MY CHILD HAS NEVER HELD A LEADERSHIP POSITION?

Leadership is the icing on the extracurricular cake. Students are rewarded for constancy and depth of interest, but leaders have a definite edge, particularly at the most selective schools where most applicants have leadership experience. It is okay for your child not to be a leader in everything. If your child has no leadership positions at all, he should look for opportunities that require initiative in his other extracurricular pursuits. For instance, he could start a new committee in an existing organization or submit stories to the local newspaper.

While some leadership is important and highly encouraged, admissions officers also appreciate a stick-to-it attitude and consistent participation. Remember, they value a genuine passion, such as Lily's pursuit of photography. A child shouldn't join the five-person juggling team that he has no interest in, just so he can be president. Most colleges would rather see a depth of long-term interest that did not result in a leadership position than a "quick hit" of leadership that smacks of artificiality.

Example 3: The Passionately Focused Young Adult

Sam was a highly accomplished thespian. He participated in his school's extensive theater program both on stage and behind the scenes. He organized a cabaret at his church. He participated in stand-up comedy nights at school, as well as the annual talent shows. On weekends he took acting classes in a nearby city, and during the summers, he participated in summer stock community theater. His passion was evident, and he continuously looked for ways to further develop it, expand upon it, and continue to challenge himself.

The above example could apply to a student who is equally passionate about computers, Chinese history, or virtually any other topic. The key factor is commitment. Don't be afraid to show that your child has a deep interest in one area. Remember, colleges are looking for a well-rounded student *body*, which includes room for students with singular but deeply felt interests.

DON'T PANIC! WHAT IF MY CHILD IS UNFOCUSED, OR "CLUELESS," ABOUT HIS INTERESTS?

If your child really isn't sure what college major or career he aspires to, and he has tried multiple electives, after-school activities, and summer programs, then look for themes and talents in his diverse résumé and build on those with course selection and additional extracurriculars. For instance, if he has worked on the school paper, excels in history, interned at a law firm, and cheers on the pep squad, instead of positioning him as well-rounded to colleges, you could tell a story of a boy with excellent communications talent. This pulls together the themes of written and oral communication and paints a more cohesive picture. If this child is a sophomore or junior, you might encourage him to seek a leadership position on the school newspaper and try a public speaking class on the weekends to improve his overall extracurricular profile.

The examples above demonstrate commitment, energy, responsibility, leadership, and pursuit of natural interests. There is no perfect combination for success, no "right" number of activities, and no guarantees for admission. But each student benefited in the college admissions process from extracurricular pursuits. The students pursued natural interests, had a sense of what they believed in, and knew a bit about their future intentions. And they surely had almost no trouble identifying several topics for their college essays.

These profiles, though above average, are not unattainable and would be quite common among applicants to selective colleges. Some parents worry that the only students who get into college have done something completely extraordinary, like developing a cure for a rare disease, learning to speak Farsi, or starring in a play on Broadway. But as you can see, Dylan, Lily, and Sam each participated in school-based activities and supplemented those experiences with out-of-school pursuits that can be found in most communities.

And in each situation, adults at school and in the community became familiar with the strength and reputation of the student. This can be an enormous asset when it comes time to select faculty members for letters of recommendation. When a teacher or counselor can speak not just of the student's contributions to the classroom, but also to the school and community as a whole, it creates a more interesting picture, which, in turn provides a greater impact on the college admissions evaluation process.

III. REPUTATION

Students should work to develop a positive reputation in high school, to supplement their academic and extracurricular record and profile. Your child's reputation at school, particularly among adults, is the final piece of the high school picture an admissions officer will assess. Students who develop healthy relationships with their peer group and positive relationships with other adults have the most rewarding and satisfying high school career—and a better chance of getting into their college of choice. Kids without worthwhile connections are frequently unhappy, less involved in meaningful activities, disconnected from their community, and often do not achieve academic potential. As a parent, there is much you can do to help your child earn respect and admiration throughout high school.

Helping Your Child Become a School Citizen

For an admissions officer at a selective school, one of the main objectives is to create a picture of the applicant as a school citizen. In other words: What type of kid is this? Would this boy be a good roommate, lab partner, community leader? Will this girl be involved in a sorority, community service, athletics, or peer tutoring?

Remember that, in addition to selecting students to attend their school, admissions officers are creating a community of people. The extracurricular profile and essay will supply some of this information, but the most powerful statements about this involvement will probably come from a teacher, coach, or adviser in the form of a recommendation. Therefore, to maximize the high school experience and prepare for the college application process, students should develop a few substantial relationships with teachers or other adults at the high school. This is particularly important if your child is currently a freshman, sophomore, or junior.

Almost all parents I've worked with have a sense of their child's reputation at school, from report card comments, parent-teacher meetings, and intuition. If you have any doubts, contact your child's guidance counselor to discuss this important issue. If, after assessing your child's reputation, you think it needs some work, here are some actions you can suggest to your child to improve relationships at school:

- Be polite to all students and adults
- Obey the rules during school hours and after-school events.
- Attend school events, such as sports tournaments, school dances, and pep rallies.
- Act like a role model to younger kids, perhaps through tutoring, interaction on sports teams, or socially by having friends in all grades.

Some other, less obvious, suggestions include:

- Volunteer on an existing school committee.
- Create a new extracurricular activity.
- Help plan an event, such as an art show, a school-wide fundraiser, or new student orientation.

As a former high school administrator primarily responsible for student activities and student life, I saw kids distinguish themselves in positive and negative ways. I noticed who said hello to other kids in the hallway, who held the doors for the people behind them, who handed in permission slips on time. I knew who would be helpful during homecoming or if I needed a quick favor. I wasn't the only one who noticed; other faculty members did too. We talked over lunch, sharing stories about students who stood out in both good and bad ways. It's important to understand that throughout high school, students are building a reputation with the adults they see daily. Students should be genuine but also aware that teachers and administrators are watching, talking, and remembering.

Note that any of the recommendations mentioned in this section can have a positive impact during all four years of high school—even first semester senior year before college applications are due. If your child's attempt to improve a poor reputation is genuine and earnest, it is never too late to become a respected school citizen.

IV. PARENT TO-DO: GOAL SETTING

Now that I have explored the three key components of your child's high school experience—academics, extracurricular activities, and reputation—it is time to work with your child to put a detailed plan into action. This final section of Chapter 1 offers the tangible tools and support you will need to help your child apply all of the information presented so far. There are many conversations you can have and exercises you can complete to help your child survive and thrive throughout high school and during the college admissions process. It's all about communication, honesty, and strategy.

I know that talking to a teenager about college and the future isn't always easy. Some kids are excited about the college admissions process, and others are scared to death by the fierce competition, the endless choices, and a natural fear of growing up. As a parent, it's your job to open the lines of communication. Here are some tips to keep in mind.

- The "let's talk about college" conversation shouldn't come out of left field. If you aren't in the habit of regularly speaking to your child about important issues (other than negotiating curfew), it's a good idea to ease into the process by talking about other things first. You may ask your son what he thinks about a particular world event in the news or suggest that he tell you about some interesting things he's been learning in history class. Solicit your child's opinions, so he will know that it's okay to share honest thoughts and dreams about the future.
- Share some fun activities with your child to build trust and communication, especially if you haven't "hung out" together in

a while. Ask your daughter what she wants to do with you, such as attending a soccer match or getting a manicure. These fun times can serve as a good chance to casually introduce the topic of college and goal setting for the future. Take cues from your child on where and when to talk. Some teens will open up on a quiet walk, while others prefer to talk over a burger and fries.

- Whenever you are having a conversation with your child, particularly about college and the future, listen more than you talk. Don't belittle his ideas, roll your eyes, or take a phone call while you're talking. The more a parent listens honestly and without judgment, the more a child is likely to share.

TO-DO: GOAL-SETTING EXERCISE

In high school, it is important for students to think about setting goals, since clear goals can influence the choices they make. For example, I am currently working with a tenth grader, Steve, who is working toward three goals: all-league in his sport, achieving grades of B+ or better, and adding one additional extracurricular activity to his busy schedule. If he achieves these goals, he will be on track for his selected schools.

Steve could play a Division III sport if he continues to improve and works diligently in the off-season. He also knows that as a recruited athlete, he might have a slight edge in the admissions process. As a result, this year he chose to take slightly less rigorous courses and will do the same next year. His goal is to maintain high grades and still manage his athletic commitments. Instead of taking an AP course load, he maintained a challenging all-honors curriculum, a manageable and not overwhelming schedule. Looking at his athletic and academic results so far this year, he seems to have made the right choice. Goal setting also provides a sense of satisfaction and confidence. Steve can focus on the activities that are productive and make him happy, while helping him realize what he wants to accomplish for the remainder of high school.

Goal setting is important, because it will help your child understand himself better. Your child should think about his current activities and where he wants to spend his time. As an involved parent, you can help your child brainstorm (preferably starting in ninth grade) about high school and future goals. With concrete goals in mind—such as maintaining a strong GPA and achieving extracurricular milestones like an athletic honor or a place in a prestigious art exhibit—your child's decisions surrounding the high school experience become easier because he is narrowing his choices to those that interest him and fit with his profile as a student committed to certain activities or skills.

Here are some general guidelines to suggest to your child when beginning the process of goal setting.

- Write down your goals so you have a record of your thoughts.
- Share your goals with someone, preferably an adult, to determine if they are challenging enough or perhaps too challenging.
- Check in with your goals periodically, perhaps once a month or once a semester, to assess on your progress.
- Adjust if necessary; nothing is set in stone.
- Be realistic.
- Have your goals reflect what really makes you happy.
- Be creative—try new things.
- Don't focus on grades alone.
- Be specific, concrete, and positive.

Once you've set up these basic guidelines, you can begin to help your child get more specific. The following questions can help define your child's goal setting through the first three years of high school.

1. What are three goals I want to accomplish by the end of the first semester this year? Considering my goals, what are three specific steps I can take to make each a reality?
2. What are three goals I want to accomplish by the end of

this school year? What specific steps, in addition to the steps above, can I take to make this happen?

3. What are my longer-term goals? What would I like to accomplish by high school graduation? What specific steps do I need to take in order to achieve each goal by the end of high school?

The following examples demonstrate sample goal setting sheets, including my commentary, for the first three years of high school.

Example 1: Goal-Setting Sheet for Ninth Grade Student

Goals I want to accomplish by the end of the first semester: Note that setting goals for first semester is a valuable exercise for ninth graders with no experience of the high school environment. These were established the summer before freshman year.

1. Earn all As.
This is an admirable goal but might be setting sights too high; better to be specific, "Earn an A in honors English, my best subject."
2. Make two new friends.
This is a great goal for a ninth grader, and an important one, too. You should value this type of goal as much as you would one about academics. Make sure your child understands that his happiness is as important as his success in the classroom.
3. Write two articles for the school paper.
This is another great goal—specific, achievable, perhaps risky, but could yield big benefits down the road.

Goals I want to achieve by the end of freshman year:

1. Qualify for honors classes in sophomore year.
2. Find a regular babysitting job.
3. Run for an editorial position on newspaper for tenth grade.

These are all good—positive, specific, doable. Each one can be achieved by following a specific plan of action.

Goals I want to achieve by high school graduation:

1. Get into dream school A.
2. Get academic scholarship to private school B.
3. Be class president.

All good, except the class president seems to come out of left field. If this is a true goal, then perhaps some work in student government would be a good first step as a ninth grader. He will see if he likes the activity and will get one step closer to this longer-term goal.

Example 2: Goal-Setting Sheet for Tenth Grade Student

A student established these goals during the summer before sophomore year.

Goals I want to achieve by the end of sophomore year:
1. **Get better grades.**
Too vague—this led to a conversation where we defined "better" and what was reasonable. We decided that he would change this to "All final grades of B+ and better."
2. **Join a club.**
Again, too vague. This led to conversation in which we identified several areas of interest and decided he would attend the first meetings of student government, newspaper, and robotics club.
3. **Make the county wrestling tournament.**
This was great—specific, doable, and concrete.

Goals I want to achieve by high school graduation:
1. **Have a high GPA.**
Again, this leads to a good conversation about what "high" and "reasonable" means. What are you shooting for?
2. **Get into a good college.**
This is a good jumping-off point for a family conversation about what a "good college" is and what that means to all of you.
3. **Become captain of the wrestling team.**
Specific and doable as well as a great motivator.

Example 3: Goal-Setting Sheet for Eleventh Grade Student

A student established these following goals during the summer before junior year.

Goals I want to achieve by end of third quarter junior year:
1. **Maintain B+ or better in chemistry.**
   a. Study for every test.
   b. Do homework/hand in every assignment on time.
2. **Maintain B or better in pre-calculus.**
   a. Study a lot for tests.
   b. Go for help if I do not understand something.
3. **Date for junior prom.**

This student has given himself excellent goals, as well as taken it to the next level and identified ways to get himself there. Number 3 should not be diminished—this is a serious social goal for this particular student, though he did not share with me his ideas on how he might accomplish it!

Goals I want to achieve by the end of junior year:
1. **Make new friend.**
   a. Talk to new people.
   b. Be more outgoing.
   c. Sit with new people at lunch.
2. **Earn over 75 on all statewide tests.**
   a. Study hard.
   b. Pay attention in class/take good notes.
   c. Ask for help if I do not understand.
3. **All grades B or better on fourth-quarter report card.**
   a. Hand in all work on time.
   b. Talk to teachers and get extra help if I need it.
   c. Do not procrastinate.

Once again, great ideas on how to get there. I suggested this student post this somewhere in his house where he would see it at least once per day, ideally in the morning, to remind himself of the action steps he wants to take. If the student shares this with his parents, they will begin to have a better sense of his social struggles and what he might be worried about in addition to his academic performance.

Goals I want to achieve by high school graduation:
1. Pass road test.
    a. Pay attention in driver's ed class.
    b. Listen to driving instructor.
    c. Practice what I learn on road with parents.
    d. Study rules and regulations.
Although this might not be the most intense or ambitious goal, it's clearly important to this student. The way he has laid out a careful, thoughtful, and specific game plan led to a conversation about how he can use this determination in other areas of his life, and how he can similarly plan for more lofty goals.

2. Get a car.
    a. Maintain B and higher grades.
    b. Complete goal 1.
    c. Be nice to parents.
When I read this, it was immediately clear to me that a car had been a carrot hung over this student's head for some time. Be careful how you determine what rewards will be and how you will decide if a student receives them. This has become such a preoccupation for this kid that he's making it one of his major goals for high school graduation—and it's arguable whether or not he really even needs to work for it.

3. Get into college.
    a. Maintain good grades.
Be more specific! Use third quarter goals as a model.
    b. Participate in more extracurricular activities.
As in the case of the tenth grader, we needed to talk about what exactly this student could and was willing to do between now and high school graduation. This is an important piece of his applications and one he still had time to salvage, so this goal became an important one to flesh out.
    c. Volunteer; do more community service.
This student had participated in and enjoyed his previous service activities and wanted to complete more, for both the personal satisfaction, learning,

and experiences, and as a way to define himself [once it came time to complete] the college applications.

DON'T PANIC! WHAT IF MY CHILD IS A SENIOR? IS IT TOO LATE TO SET SOME GOALS?

If your child is a senior, it *is* too late to spend time setting goals about extracurriculars, courses, and leadership positions. But it is *not* too late to do the introspective thinking and writing that accompany goal setting. Here are two suggestions.

1. Rather than trying to set high school-related goals at this late stage, it's better to spend time developing a theme out of your child's existing high school experience. (Note that there are many questions to help you develop a theme in Chapter 5.) This process will help your child develop self-awareness as well as an application strategy that will benefit him throughout the college selection process, essays, and interviews.

2. Because the practice of goal setting is important to learn and will benefit your child once he arrives at college, you might also take some time to help your child set postsecondary goals—for the summer after graduation and the first year or two of college. Again, this helps your child develop self-awareness and will also come in handy when he is asked the inevitable interview question, "What are your future plans?"

Congratulations on surviving the high school experience! If you are the parent of an underclassman, I encourage you to refer back to this chapter when you face curriculum-and activity-related decisions over the next few years. If you are the parent of a senior, then you can breathe a sigh of relief that this stage of the process is nearly complete.

CHAPTER 2

STANDARDIZED TESTS

Expert Coach: Brooke Stengel Fitzgerald, Former Admissions Officer, Columbia University

Few aspects of the college admissions process bring out as much anxiety as the taking of standardized tests. Think back to your own experience of the SAT and you're likely to recall sweaty palms, broken pencil points, and the nerve-wracking moment of opening the envelope with your scores.

The good news is that this chapter offers many strategies for easing your child's anxiety over test taking. The bad news is that today's high school students face an extra challenge: in 2005, the "New SAT" was launched, and the ramifications to the college admissions process are still somewhat unclear. In this chapter, you will find key information and tips about this new test, known as the SAT I, as well as other standardized tests, including the PSAT, ACT, SAT II, and AP exams.

There are dozens of test prep booklets, guides, and Web sites you can access for specific help in studying for and taking exams; I'll recommend a few on the following pages. But for the purposes of this book, my goal is to show you how each standardized test fits into your child's overall college application strategy. As you will see, a little test planning—including which tests to take, when to take them, and what scores to report to which colleges—can go a very long way in reducing stress and maximizing success.

RULES TO REMEMBER IN THIS CHAPTER

- **Start researching tests early and plan, plan, plan.** Early in high school it is crucial to understand college testing requirements so your child can make informed decisions on which standardized exams he will take, when he should take them, and the options to report his scores to colleges.
- **Become an exam expert.** Every standardized test has a different purpose, scoring system, preparation strategy, and meaning to colleges. Learn as much as you can about each test to help your child make the best decisions for his particular skills and college application plans.

I. THE BASICS

How important are standardized test scores to an admissions officer today? The answer varies from school to school and from student to student, but admissions officers do consider the following factors when looking at a student's scores:

- **Can the test scores serve as a tiebreaker?** If two or more students of relatively equal grades and activities are applying from the same high school, then test scores can be the deciding factor. Admissions officers can make a decision based on this measurable difference.
- **Will this student's scores help our college's admissions statistics?** Colleges want their incoming class to have the highest possible SAT average in hopes of boosting their position on the national ranking lists, thereby improving their applicant recruiting power for the subsequent year. Although admissions officers don't like to admit it, they do pay attention to the reputation of their college when deciding which students to admit. Higher scores of admitted students can accomplish this, particularly if a school is in the process of repositioning itself as more competitive.

There are some exceptions. Recruited athletes, legacies (students with a family member who attended the school), and minorities are sometimes held to a different test score standard. But it is safest to assume that your child's test scores will be assessed in the same way as other applicants'.

The Testing Timeline

Because high school students are faced with a dizzying number of standardized tests, test dates, and reporting options, your first task is to make sense of it all. The sooner you start marking dates on your calendar, the better. Here is a sample chart, mapping out my suggested timeline for preparing and taking tests. The following sections will describe each test in detail.

Grade 10	
Fall	Register for PSAT (optional).
	Take PSAT in October (optional).
	Begin to think about which SAT IIs to take.
Spring	Register for SAT IIs, if applicable, based on the student's school courses.
	Take SAT IIs, if applicable.
Summer	SAT test preparation recommended.

Grade 11	
Fall	Register for PSAT.
	Take PSAT in October.
Spring	Register for SAT I or ACT, and SAT IIs, if applicable.
	SAT preparation, if applicable.
	Take SAT I or ACT for the first time, and SAT IIs, if applicable.
Summer	Test preparation if the student wants to retake the SAT in the fall to improve his scores.

Grade 12	
Fall	Register for SAT I or ACT and SAT II for the second time, if necessary.
	Take/retake SAT I or ACT and SAT II, if necessary.
Spring	Take AP exams, if applicable.

II. THE PSAT: PRELIMINARY SCHOLASTIC ACHIEVEMENT TEST

What Is the PSAT?

A student's exposure to college-level standardized testing begins in tenth or eleventh grade with the Preliminary Scholastic Achievement Test, or PSAT. The three sections of the PSAT—critical reading, math, and writing—are exactly the same length and difficulty as the sections on the new SAT I, but they are scored out of 80 points. Simply putting a zero on the end of each section score provides an estimated SAT I score—for example, a PSAT writing score of 62 would equate to an SAT writing score of 620. The PSAT is only administered in October, and both the registration and administration are handled by the student's high school. Many high schools require eleventh-grade students to take the test, and some will offer it to tenth-grade students who would like the practice. PSAT test scores are *not* considered as part of the college admissions process, but students' PSAT scores often provide a good indication of what future SAT scores will be. Therefore, it is important to include the PSAT in a smart college admissions strategy.

What Is the Best PSAT Test Strategy?

1. If possible, take the PSAT for practice in tenth grade

Some schools do not offer the PSAT to tenth graders due to time or space constraints, but if your school does offer this opportunity, your child should take it. (If your school does not offer this option, you might want to contact another school in your area.)

Here are the reasons why:

- It's great practice. Since no one will see the tenth grade PSAT scores and the cost is minimal (around $12), there is really no reason not to get used to the test and the testing atmosphere.
- It's good information. Your child will receive the PSAT test booklet with his scores, so he can review his answer, the right answer, and any notes or formulas he jotted down. This is a great learning tool for future exams.

2. Prepare for the eleventh grade PSAT

Even though PSAT scores do not count toward college admissions, I recommend that students prepare for the exam. While it is not necessary to prepare for the PSAT to the same extent a student would prepare for the important SAT, here are the reasons why moderate preparation (taking a few practice tests and/or reading a PSAT prep book) are beneficial.

- If your child does prepare for the PSAT, his score will be a better predictor of his SAT I, since he will undoubtedly prepare for that exam.
- A strong PSAT score can really boost a child's confidence and inspire that child to study thoroughly for the SAT.
- There are, however, some possible downsides to consider. If your student chooses not to prepare for the PSAT and scores poorly, he may lose confidence in his testing ability once the SAT test comes around.
- It's unfortunate, but gossip happens among teenagers, so kids can be labeled "smart" or "dumb" based on their PSAT scores. This can also undermine a child's confidence early in the test-taking cycle.

3. Understand the National Merit Scholarship

While the PSAT is not a required admissions test, students who achieve the highest scores in the country are named National Merit Scholarship Commended Scholars, Semifinalists and, ultimately, Finalists. National Merit is an outstanding honor and may result in scholarship opportunities during the college application process. Countrywide, less than 1 percent of graduating high school seniors qualify as Semifinalists, so only a rare few will qualify.

If you believe your child may achieve such a remarkable score, then you may want to discuss a more aggressive preparation strategy with your school's guidance counselor. This is, of course, an impressive distinction to list on a college application. Unfortunately, there is no designated range of scores to qualify for a National Merit Scholarship, so there are no guarantees. The cutoff score is based upon national averages; therefore, the minimum score to qualify for Merit Scholarships varies from year to year based upon the national range. To learn more about the scholarship, requirements, and how to participate, you can consult the National Merit Scholarship Corporation's Web site at www. nationalmerit.org.

What Are Colleges Looking for in the PSAT Score?

As mentioned, the PSAT is primarily a practice test for the SAT I and is *not* considered as part of the college admissions process.

III. THE SAT I: SCHOLASTIC ACHIEVEMENT TEST

What Is the SAT I?

The Scholastic Achievement Test is the most well known, most commonly taken test in the college admissions process. The SAT I (aka the New SAT) is a timed (three hour and forty-five minutes) reasoning test that measures critical reading skills (determining what is editorially and grammatically correct), mathematical aptitude, and writing ability. The writing component is the newest: the College Board added this section to reinforce the importance of writing skills throughout a student's education, and as a result, to support the improvement of students' preparedness for writing at the college level.

Let's look, section by section, at how the SAT I differs from the "old" SAT.

- **Critical Reading** (formerly called the Verbal section). Total time: 70 minutes. This portion of the test consists of two 25-minute sections and one 20-minute section. Critical Reading includes: sentence completion, reading comprehension, and analysis of short, paragraph-long passages. This portion of the SAT is geared toward measuring a student's understanding of word definitions, sentence organization, vocabulary in context, reasoning skills, and overall comprehension. The analogies section has been eliminated.

- **Math.** Total time: 70 minutes. This portion consists of two 25-minute sections and one 20-minute section. The Math component of the test includes: linear functions, geometry, statistics, data analysis, probabilities, and now algebra II questions. The section, comprised of both multiple-choice and student-produced answers, is geared toward measuring overall number sense and estimating abilities. The quantitative comparison questions have been eliminated. Students may use a calculator for this portion of the exam.

- **Writing.** Total time: 60 minutes. The new writing section consists of 35 minutes of multiple-choice and 25 minutes for a written essay. The multiple-choice questions include: grammar, usage, word choice, subject-verb agreement, and diction to measure a student's ability to identify and improve errors. The essay assesses proper word usage, sentence structure, development of thoughts and ideas, as well as clarity and overall organization. In the essay, students should discuss their point of view using experience or reason. Two readers review the essay, grading it on a 1-6 scale; therefore, a student will receive a combined score of 2-12, which is included in the overall writing score and also appears on your child's test results as a subscore.

The essay is handwritten, so encourage your student to write legibly. There are no extra points for penmanship, but you wouldn't want to lose points because a grader can't read your child's handwriting!

What happens to the essays in the writing section after they are scored? Colleges are able to access them online to use for admissions purposes, course placement, and to replace or supplement application essays. Perhaps most important, colleges can use the SAT essay to confirm the authenticity of a submitted college application essay based on level, style, and other factors.

But don't worry too much about the fact that colleges might see your child's SAT essay. It is relatively rare for a school to do this, unless there is a huge discrepancy between the SAT writing essay score and the level of the application essay. The other time the SAT essay might be accessed is when a student is considered borderline and the essay could tip the scales. Admissions officers are busy, so they will only review the online SAT essay if they consider it absolutely necessary.

When it comes to scoring the entire exam, the new SAT is scored like the old SAT: each of the three sections is scored out of 800 points. However, at the time of the writing of this book, it is unknown whether the essay will be evaluated as an additional component to the Critical Reading and Math section, or whether all three sections will be assessed together. Some colleges are indicating they will consider scores on the full 2,400-point scale (800 for Critical Reading, 800 for Math, and 800 for Writing), while others feel more comfortable maintaining the scale at 1600 for the Math and Critical Reading, plus an additional 800 points for the Writing section.

Note that the national average SAT score falls at approximately 500 points scored per section. To stay up-to-date on all issues related to the SAT and its scoring, refer to the College Board Web site at www.collegeboard.com. This is also a good resource for sample test questions.

WARNING!

It is fair to say that the new SAT is more challenging and stressful than the old SAT. First, the new test is 35 minutes longer—no small issue when the test already required a marathon effort. Second, the addition of the Writing section, which is somewhat abstract and difficult to "study" for, can cause additional anxiety. The fact that the College Board is still working out the kinks of questions and scoring also adds to the challenge. The good news is that the College Board is not trying to hide anything or trick students—its Web site, www.collegeboard.com, highlights all of the changes clearly. Change is never easy, but keep in mind that the test is new for all students, so your child is no worse off than anyone else.

What Is the Best SAT I Strategy?

The SAT I is usually given seven times per year on a Saturday. Exact test dates, registration fees, and other basic information can be found on the College Board Web site. High school guidance offices have forms for SAT registration by mail, though most students register online. The SAT I has two deadlines for registration: one regular deadline and one "last chance" deadline, which includes an increased fee. Be very aware of when these dates occur; you don't want your child to miss out on a chance to take or retake this very important exam. Ideally, your child should register four to six weeks before the test.

As you saw in the testing timeline at the beginning of this chapter, I recommend that students take the SAT I for the first time in the late winter or spring of eleventh grade. The reason is that if the first set of scores are disappointing, students can study some more and retake the exam in the fall of twelfth grade. If your daughter gets a low score on the Critical Reading section but scores well in other areas, then she can focus on preparing more for that one, weak section. To be safe, a student should never wait until the fall of twelfth grade to take any test for the first time. You always want to have the option of retaking the test for the best possible scores. Note that more than half of all SAT takers sit for the exam more than once and admissions officers don't penalize students for multiple tries.

Preparation for the SAT I is absolutely, no question, totally, completely essential. Because the SAT I is an aptitude test that is not directly related to high school curriculum, students must prepare for the test outside of school hours. Here are my answers to some frequently asked questions about SAT test prep strategy:

Q: What kind of SAT test prep is best?

A: There are hundreds of books, courses, private tutors, and on-line resources to help students in this area, and I encourage you to find the resource that is best suited to your child, his ambitions, and your budget. For local recommendations, speak with other parents in your area and teachers at your child's school. As you know, students learn in different ways, so some prefer private tutoring, some thrive in a group class, and others would rather prepare through a computer software program. Sometimes the best strategy is a combination. Do whatever works for your child and keeps him motivated and improving.

Q: What is the ideal time, and length of time, to prepare for the SAT I?

A: I advise most students to begin preparing for the SAT the summer between sophomore and junior years. Good test prep takes time, and spending a bulk of time studying in the summer means that regular schoolwork will not get in the way. Students also feel more relaxed in the summer and generally less anxious about test taking. As I have mentioned, it is ideal for all students to take the SAT I in eleventh grade, in case they need to retake the exam again in the fall of senior year. This strategy also means that the student can complete additional prep the summer between eleventh and twelfth grades.

Q: If my child resists studying or the test is too soon for a full prep course, what can we do?

A: I am a strong believer in focused studying, particularly when students are working within a short time frame. For instance, if math is more of a problem for your son, then he should spend time focusing on math. Students should also be sure to practice taking the test in full, to prepare for the experience of taking such a long exam. You can find many books that offer full-length SAT I practice tests for this purpose.

What Are Colleges Looking for in the SAT I Score?

Once you understand how the SAT I exam works and when to take the test, it is important to know how colleges will review your student's scores. To be blunt, the SAT (along with the ACT, described in detail below) is the most important exam and the first scores an admissions officer will notice. However, college applications ask for the student's best score on each SAT section, even if the scores were achieved on different dates. When evaluating a student's application, admissions officers look at the highest *composite* score. Although they will *see* every score, they will honestly give a student the benefit of the doubt and consider only the best scores. This shows effort to improve on the student's behalf.

DON'T PANIC! WHAT IF MY CHILD'S SAT I SCORES ARE MUCH LOWER THAN THE AVERAGE SCORES AT HIS DESIRED SCHOOL?

Disappointing SAT I scores are a reality for many families. The first thing to remember is that SAT scores are only one element of the college application process. They are important, yes, but they are one piece of the puzzle. Here are some realistic strategies for dealing with lower than desired scores:

- If there is another opportunity to take the exam, make preparation time more of a priority and take the test again. A bad score could just be the result of a bad day. This is particularly important if your child's practice test scores were much higher than his actual scores.

- Focus your child's time and energy on other elements of the application that are in his control. Work twice as hard to make application essays shine, acquire stellar recommendations, and prepare for a strong interview.
- Adjust your child's expectations about which schools are realistic possibilities given the lower scores. In many cases, you can find less competitive schools that offer a similar environment to your child's "dream" schools. (For much more on this topic, see Chapter 3.)
- Consider taking the ACT (see section below).

IV. THE SAT II SUBJECT TESTS

What Is the SAT II?

The SAT IIs (formerly called the Achievement Tests) are timed, one-hour exams that test a student's knowledge of a particular academic subject. Many highly selective colleges and universities require two or three SAT II tests in different subjects. Be sure to check each college's requirements since some colleges may suggest an applicant to take specific exams, while other schools allow the student to choose. Note that the term "Achievement Test" is no longer used.

With the introduction of the new SAT I, which includes a Writing portion, there will no longer be an SAT II in Writing. Since many colleges once required the writing subject test, it is more common today for colleges only to require two SAT IIs. The remaining twenty-two subject areas include math, American history, world history, French, Spanish, German, Latin, biology, chemistry, and physics, among others. The SAT II exams, like the SAT I, are scored out of 800 points. As with the SAT I, registration information for the SAT II is available on the College Board Web site or in your high school guidance office.

What Is the Best SAT II Strategy?

1. Decide *when* your child should take each SAT II

While I recommend that students take the SAT I during the latter half of their junior year or the beginning of their senior year of high school, the SAT II subject tests can be taken at any time during your child's high school career. Although it is pretty unusual for a freshman to take an SAT II, you should think about the SAT II subject exams as early as possible during high school because course work can help them prepare for the exams. Students should take an SAT II test after they have completed the highest level of the corresponding course or as advised by their teachers.

For example, if your son is taking advanced U.S. history as a second-semester tenth grader, it may be best for him to take the U.S. history subject test in June of that year. The material will be fresh in his mind and he will prepare for the SAT II by studying for his class final exam.

On the other hand, if your daughter has taken advanced French courses throughout high school, it is probably best to wait until June of eleventh grade to take this particular test. That way, she will have expanded her vocabulary and knowledge base right up until the test date.

Students may also take an SAT II subject test more than once. For example, many students will take the biology SAT II at the end of tenth grade after completing intro to biology. However, if a student decides to take an advanced biology course in eleventh or twelfth grade, retaking the SAT II exam will likely yield a higher score. As with the SAT I scores, the admissions committee will most likely focus on the higher of the two scores. However, the committee may also decide to look at the more recent exam as a representation of the student's current academic performance. So I only recommend taking the second biology exam if a child is confident his score will be equally good or better than the tenth grade score.

2. Decide *which* SAT IIs your child should take and when

Ultimately, your child should choose which SAT IIs to take based on his comfort level with the subject matter. Colleges used to require writing and two other subjects, but now students may choose all three subjects. In my experience, the most commonly taken SAT II subjects are math and history. To determine what is right for your child, try this simple four-step strategy:

- **Evaluate.** Look closely at class grades and class level (e.g., honors) to determine your child's strongest subject areas each year.
- **Compare.** Ask subject teachers how previous students with similar grades to your child's have done on that subject's SAT II.
- **Review.** A few months before the SAT II exam, look through a review book for each subject exam to gauge your child's ability to answer the questions correctly.
- **Research.** Check the application requirements of the colleges your child is considering, even though his choices may change over time.

As an aside, I have found that some SAT II subject exams are more challenging than others, even within the same subject. For instance, even students who are fluent in a foreign language find the listening component of the SAT II language exams to be a challenge. However, the foreign language SAT IIs are usually given without the listening component, so check testing dates for exact details. Language test dates are designated as "reading only" or "reading and listening." Try to take the test without the listening component; it is not required.

3. Prepare

Although there are similarities, high school courses are not taught to the SAT II exams, so students cannot rely solely on high school curriculum for preparation. There are some prep courses and tutors for the SAT IIs, but they are not as common as for the SAT. The best preparation is for students to familiarize themselves with the exams by taking practice tests in review books, that can be found at most bookstores.

What Are Colleges Looking for in the SAT II Score?

SAT II scores help college admissions officers confirm students' strengths in particular subject areas. At specialized colleges, such as engineering schools that require applicants to take SAT IIs in chemistry or physics, specific tests help to show the admissions officer the strength of the high school curriculum. Be especially careful when you are applying to a specialized school, as you need to score strongly in the specialized area in order to stand out as an applicant.

Keep in mind that, unlike the SAT I where students choose which scores to send to colleges, admissions officers will see *all* SAT II scores. In most cases, if a student takes a particular SAT II subject exam more than once, the college admissions officer will record only the highest score, even though he has scores for multiple attempts. If a student must submit scores from two SAT II exams, but they have taken four different subject tests, the admissions committee will likely place the strongest emphasis on the two highest subject scores, unless certain tests are required as part of the student's prospective major (for instance, a student who is very serious about majoring in engineering should take math and science SAT IIs).

Unless a student is taking a fourth exam to make up for a poor score in an earlier SAT II exam, there is no advantage to taking more than three SAT II exams. It's really not a good use of a student's time. He is better off studying for school classes, completing college applications, or taking some much-needed rest from the pressures of high school!

V. THE ACT: AMERICAN COLLEGE TEST

What Is the ACT?

The ACT is a timed, 3-hour-and-25-minute multiple-choice test that assesses knowledge in four areas: English (covering usage, mechanics, and rhetorical skills), reading (assessing ability to comprehend and answer questions about paragraphs), mathematics (including algebra, trigonometry, and geometry), and science (understanding graphs, experiment summaries, and research viewpoints). There is also a 30-minute writing section, which is optional. However, about four hundred colleges and universities require the writing section, so I recommend that students go ahead and opt to take it. Before taking the ACT, be sure to check if a college on your student's list requires or recommends the optional writing test. It also costs more to register for the ACT plus writing portion, so students must decide if they are taking the writing section before the testing date. If a student takes the ACT in lieu of the New SAT, which requires a writing portion, it is best for the student to take the ACT writing section. All information regarding the ACT, test dates, and school requirements can be found at www.act.org.

What Is the Best ACT Strategy?

The most important question regarding ACT strategy is really about whether to take the test instead of the SAT I. Your child can even take both tests to see which one he scores better on. But most students do not want to take additional tests if it's unnecessary, so how can a student determine which exam to take? Here are some issues to consider when making the decision with your child.

- **Alignment with high school curriculum.** Students who are strong academically will often have to prepare less for the ACT, since the test is better aligned to a high school curriculum. Consequently, many, but not all, students find the ACT exam easier than the SAT. Therefore, if your child has done well in class, there is a good chance that he will do well on the ACT. More and more guidance counselors and families are realizing the benefits of the ACT for kids who are good students but not great testers.
- **Score reporting.** Unlike SAT reports, which show *all* of your student's scores, the ACT does not release all your student's testing dates and corresponding scores at once. When submitting

ACT scores to colleges if your child has taken the ACT more than once, you must specify exactly which record(s) and which testing date(s) you wish the ACT board to send. Colleges only will see the ACT scores you want them to see—in other words, the highest. Some applicants prefer the ACT because of this score choice option. There is no risk in taking the ACT. This usually means that students feel less anxiety about taking the test.

- **Opportunities to prepare and improve.** On the other hand, the SAT offers more room for preparation and can be manipulated with testing techniques—such as vocabulary memorization or learning to eliminate multiple-choice answers—more easily than the ACT. Keep in mind your child's strengths and willingness to prep when considering which option may be best.

- **Workload.** While some students naturally receive higher scores on the ACT than on the SAT, there is another potential benefit for taking the ACT. Selective schools often call for an applicant to submit *either* the SAT I combined with two or three SAT II subject tests, *or just the ACT*. Essentially, the ACT kills two birds with one stone. By taking the ACT, students frequently lighten their workload and stress level.

Strategy-wise, the ACT also becomes a good choice for a student who is disappointed with his SAT scores and would like a second opportunity to demonstrate his testing ability. With two sets of scores, from two very different exams, the student is able to select which exam the colleges of his choice see. If a student scores significantly higher on his ACT than on his SAT, he can choose to send only the ACT test scores to colleges and not to submit any SAT scores. This way, admissions officers will never see his low SAT numbers and he never has to worry that a college will judge him for low scores.

What Are Colleges Looking for in the ACT Score?

When making your decision about taking the ACT, be sure to check each individual college's requirements; some universities may require SAT II subject exams for course placement purposes, so the ACT alone may not be enough. But, again, most schools will consider the ACT in place of the SAT I and II. However, just as there are benefits for the ACT, do not forget that the SAT is the more widely accepted and universally known exam. Check with the colleges on your child's list to be sure of the requirements. If the ACT is accepted on its own, then you might want to seriously consider this option for your child.

VI. ADVANCED PLACEMENT (AP) TESTS

What Is the AP Exam?

Advanced Placement exams, or AP tests, usually coincide with AP classes—college-level courses in a variety of subject areas that students can take while still in high school. An AP exam serves two main purposes: first, to provide another way for colleges to assess applicants on a level playing field across high school grading systems and, second, to place out of a college course, if your student's scores are high enough.

There are thirty-four courses and exams across nineteen subject areas; exams include art history, computer science, German, statistics, and music theory. At the end of an AP course, students have the opportunity to take the corresponding AP exam. AP exams are two-to three-hour tests given in May, made up of multiple-choice and free-response essay questions, and they are graded on a scale from 1 to 5. If your child receives a qualifying grade of 3 or better on an AP exam, he may be eligible for advanced standing and credits once he gets to college. A score of 4 or 5 is considered excellent.

The AP Program also offers a number of Scholar Awards to students for outstanding performance on AP exams. This achievement is noted on the AP Grade Report and is recognized by colleges. As with the National Merit distinctions related to the PSAT, your child should definitely note if he is an AP Scholar in the academic honors section of a college application. For more information about the AP courses and exams, you can visit: http: www.collegeboard.com/student/testing/ap/about.html.

What Is the Best AP Exam Strategy?

Students should take AP exams if:

- they have taken the corresponding AP course in high school and received strong grades in the course.
- they are willing to take the time and effort to prepare for the exam and believe they will receive a score of 3 or higher.
- the AP test counts as final exam, offers college credit, and advance standing by the colleges on their lists.

When in doubt, speak to the teacher of the high school AP course to ask if your child should sit for the AP exam in that subject.

When it comes to studying, high school course work should be sufficient. There are some prep books as well. In general, students should approach AP exams as if they were studying for a final in the course.

If the schools your child wants to attend do not give college credit for AP exam grades, it is still a good idea to take the test. Sitting for AP exams, and showing a strong score, provides another example of how a student is challenging himself. This can work to your advantage in the application process. You can be quite strategic in this area. If a college does not give credit for AP exams and your child took a few tests and had mixed results, then you can opt *not* to send the AP scores directly to the school but mention the best score elsewhere on the application, perhaps in a recommendation from the teacher of that AP course.

What Are Colleges Looking for in AP Exam Scores?

For the most part, admissions officers are looking for the fact that a student made the effort to take the AP exam (or several) and excelled enough to score a 3 or better. However, if your daughter's school does not offer AP courses, she will not be penalized for not having taken them. Admissions officers do not necessarily consider the actual AP exam score; rather, they are looking for a strong curriculum throughout high school.

Each individual college ultimately determines how much credit a student receives as a result of taking the AP and for which courses. More than 1,400 institutions in the United States grant up to a full year's credit to students with qualifying grades on enough AP exams—this is called "sophomore standing." It is critical to understand that if your student does not receive a qualifying score (3 or better) on his AP exam(s), he does not have to officially report the score(s) to colleges. And although your child has the option to take an AP test more than once, students do so very rarely.

To enter freshman year with enough course credits to qualify as an academic sophomore can be financial paradise. However, students might not want to waive a college class even if they get AP credit, particularly if the course is a requirement for their major (e.g., math and science for engineers). And no matter what they say, a college-level AP course taught in high school is usually not the same as a course that is actually being taught at a college. Often, AP credit does not exempt a student from core curriculum classes. Some colleges will grant AP credit only toward elective courses—which most students want to take.

VII. OTHER IMPORTANT TESTING INFORMATION

Extended Time

If a student has learning disabilities, he may apply for arrangements that will accommodate his particular needs, including extended-timed exams. Until recently, extended-time privileges were given freely to students who demonstrated need. However, a recent College Board meeting verified that over the years too many school officials abused this policy, offering extended time to unqualified kids. Consequently, the College Board has become much stricter about requirements for applying for receiving extended time.

The plus side to the stricter policies is that extended time testing is no longer flagged on the SAT score report, since colleges sometimes discounted strong scores on extended-timed tests. Colleges will not know about the extended time unless a student tells them. There is no advantage to telling, except that students with learning disabilities should make sure colleges will accommodate their needs in some way if they attend the school.

The process of securing extended time for your child is quite formal and takes time to complete, so it should begin well in advance of the date on which your student hopes to take the test. The SAT application process is highlighted online at www.collegeboard.com/ssd and the ACT process can be found at www.act.org/aap/disab. These Web sites will help you assess whether your child has a chance to qualify. In general, most students approved for extended time are already getting accommodations in school.

To give you an idea of the requirements for SAT testing accommodations, here is list of what must be submitted to qualify:

- The Student Eligibility Form from the College Board (see www.collegeboard.com).
- A current psycho-educational evaluation. School psychologists often have a list of recommended private counselors who will administer the evaluative tests and write up the report. This costs between $2,000 and $3,000. Some public schools may have someone on staff that can conduct this extensive testing.
- Formal written documentation from the school, such as either an IEP (Individualized Education Plan) or the so-called 504 plan, which addresses only recommendations for the student's access to *regular* (not special) education.
- Proof the school has been giving the student similar testing accommodations for at least the past four months (summer school not included).

Also, like the SAT and ACT exams, certain testing accommodations can be made for the Advanced Placement exams. For more information about getting extended time accommodations when taking AP exams you can visit www.collegeboard.com.

SENDING SCORE REPORTS

Once your student has decided on a college list, he will need to request that his official exam score reports be sent to those institutions. At the time of test registration, both the SAT and ACT testing organizations will allow students to send their score reports to four colleges for free. You can request that the College Board or ACT send additional reports later in the process. You will be charged a fee for this request. These requests can be made online, by phone, or by fax. Do not pay to send score reports to any colleges until you know that your child has finished taking all of the exams that he plans to take. Colleges do not need to receive the scores right after each test is completed. Also, make sure to send the scores before application deadlines get too close, since processing requests slow as more applicants need to access the service. While rush reporting is available, it should only be used as a last resort because it is significantly more expensive.

The master SAT I and II score report lists all of the tests and scores that a student has ever taken. Remember that colleges will look at the highest SAT I section scores, even if they are not from the same testing date, as well as the highest SAT II score if a student has taken the same subject test two or more times. The best strategy with SAT reporting is to make sure to use the four free score reports during the last test your student takes. For the rest of the colleges on her list, have additional reports sent to the schools. That way you can be assured that every college received all of the scores.

Keep in mind that not all schools require standardized tests, such as Bowdoin College, Bard College, Bates College, and College of the Holy Cross. If a college of interest does not require the scores, then only send if the scores are strong relative to the scores of the general applicant pool.

As you have seen, having a standardized test strategy is tremendously important to the admissions process, but test taking does not have to cause undue stress and anxiety in your child.

CHAPTER 3

COLLEGE SELECTION

Expert Coach: Nicole Eichin,
Former Admissions Officer, College of the Holy Cross

Many college counselors talk about finding a school that is "the right fit." But how exactly do you and your child determine what school might eventually be "the one"? With around 3,700 colleges and universities in the United States, it's not easy. A comforting truth I've discovered over my career is that there are many schools out there—not just one—that can provide the right fit for your child's wants and needs, no matter how unique or choosy he may be.

The catch, of course, is that you have to determine what kind of school your child wants and needs. This takes a lot of thinking about academic needs, social interests, and the reality of admission chances at various schools. This chapter will help narrow down the 3,700 into a manageable list of seven—yes, just seven—options, divided into Dreams, Just Rights, and No Problems.

RULES TO REMEMBER IN THIS CHAPTER

- **You can get what you want.** Think hard about what your child really wants in a school, because he can have it. The key is determining a few "college list drivers" based on the most important criteria and using those most important factors to choose a selection of appropriate schools.

- **Consider life beyond the books.** Colleges must match both a student's learning *and* social style to be a strong fit.
- **Limit risk.** When seeking schools that match your child's list drivers, create an appropriate mix of schools based on likelihood of admission and selectivity. A thoughtful combination of Dreams, Just Rights, and No Problems will ensure ultimate happiness and success with the choices at the end of the admissions process.

NEW RULE OF COLLEGE ADMISSIONS: IT'S NEVER TOO EARLY

When is the right time to think about creating a list of colleges? In today's competitive college admissions climate, it is never too early. If your child is an underclassman, think about doing some window shopping to get started. You can casually look at schools where you live, or if you see a sign for a college or university while on a family vacation, drive through the campus and check it out. This can be a great starting point to compare future campus visits, brochures, and online information.

Visiting a campus with a younger student can also provide direction. For instance, when a ninth grader understands the stringent requirements he must meet in order to be admitted to a school that he thinks he loves, that can drive academic and extracurricular achievement in high school. Junior year is usually the time when families get serious about researching colleges and narrowing down choices. As I will discuss later in this chapter, visiting schools is important, but creating a list of colleges can certainly be done without visiting every school you are considering.

I. WHAT ARE YOUR CHILD'S ACADEMIC AND SOCIAL PREFERENCES?

The first step in the college selection process is to determine the criteria that will drive your child's college list. This section will guide you through a variety of factors to consider and the questions you can ask your child to create an accurate and realistic college list together.

The goal of determining selection criteria is not for your child to express a strong opinion about every single factor, but to determine which factors are most important to his potential happiness in college. At the end of this section, I will ask you to narrow down these criteria into three or four "list drivers" that are most important to your student. This will help you determine the "must-have" factors your child needs to be happy and what trade-offs might be acceptable.

As you are talking with your child about each factor below, pay attention to where his greatest interest and excitement seem to be and you will become aware of his list drivers. You may face some resistance from your child during this process, but I urge you to persevere (and perhaps use bribery, if you must). This is where the rubber meets the road in the college admissions process. The answer to these questions will help determine where you child spends the next four years of his life. Take notes in this book or on a separate sheet of paper as you are reading—each factor will be ranked on a scale of 1 to 10, as indicated in the text. Then, at the end of this section you can assess your child's ranking of each factor to come up with your list drivers.

DON'T PANIC! What if my child isn't sure what he wants?

It is completely normal for your child not to have an opinion on certain factors of the college selection process. If your child has no opinion on a particular issue, such as whether the college is suburban or rural, or whether it has an intramural tennis team, then you can simply disregard that issue as a factor in your decision making. Do not force your child to make a choice on something that is not important to him. Spend your time focusing on what really matters to your child's happiness and education, and let those factors drive the list.

Brand

A school's name brand is the very first thing you discover about it, so I address this issue up front. As we all know, many high school students are as brand conscious about colleges as they are about shoes, pocketbooks, and cars. Parents are subject to some college brand consciousness as well: I'm sure you have a gut reaction to names like Princeton, Notre Dame, Arizona State, or Wellesley based on their sports teams, famous graduates, or someone you know who attended.

I see it happen all the time that a college name will get stuck in a student's head for reasons that have nothing to do with whether the college would actually be a good fit. Many kids will want to apply to a college because a "cool" kid went there the year before, or they had a good-looking tour guide when they visited, or the college has a popular basketball team. Or, in some cases, a parent may have attended a certain school and always assumed the child would go there, too.

If you detect brand consciousness in your child's conversations about schools, I would advise that it's okay to think about brand and reputation, but don't choose a school for the name *only*. Students who attend schools just because of the name may arrive on campus and feel disappointed that the reality does not match their high expectations. Brand name should not be a list driver.

Geography

Geography is the most common driving factor. Think about it: it is about where your child will live for the next four years. Being clear on a desired geographic location can help eliminate hundreds of schools and drastically narrow down a large list of options, helping you and your child focus on more appropriate choices in more manageable numbers. There is no reason to waste time researching schools in Texas if your student doesn't want to leave your county in Michigan. If your child fears flying, you won't need to look at schools more than a drive or train ride away. I would also advise you to be aware of your own feelings about how far or near your child should travel for school.

It is important to have as open a dialogue as possible on this topic. Be sure you and your child have an understanding of what it means to go to college close to, or far from, home. Here are some questions to ask your child to help guide the conversation and decision making related to this choice:

- Is there a region of the country you'd like to explore for your future? (E.g., Los Angeles if you are interested in eventually working in the film industry, or New York if you are interested in Wall Street.)
- Do you want to go to school close to home or in a familiar place?
- How are you comfortable getting to and from school? By car, train, plane?
- Are there any parts of the country you definitely *don't* want to go to college?
- My geographic preference is _____.
- On a scale of 1 to 10, how important is a school's geographic location to your decision:_____.

Setting

There are pros and cons to any college setting—city, suburb, or rural. Often I find that students, even if they are not entirely sure, tend to lean either city/suburb or suburb/rural. You should encourage your child to think about this factor in the context of where you live now. If your family lives in New York City, attending a rural school could be shocking for your daughter if she has never experienced that environment. Or a boy from a small town could be overwhelmed by an urban university. When thinking about your child, and activities outside of the classroom they enjoy, you want to ensure the college town offers opportunities to build upon those interests.

If your child really isn't sure, here are some questions to determine which setting might be best. If your child really doesn't care, then this will not be a list driver for your family.

- Do you want to be in a setting—urban, suburban, or rural—that is similar to or different from where you are now?
- Do you want to be near nature, out in the country?
- Would you rather be in an environment where school activities are the main social scene, or do you want to interact with a larger community (malls, museums, theater, dance clubs, et cetera)?
- Are you interested in community service work in an urban environment, like tutoring at an inner-city school? Or would you be interested in volunteering in a rural area, such as building homes or working with animals?
- My setting preference is: _____.
- On a scale of 1 to 10, how important is a school's setting to your decision? _____.

Size

Schools, like college logo T-shirts, come in three basic sizes: small, medium, and large. Even if your child is not totally sure, I find that most students tend to lean toward either small/medium or medium/large.

Academic needs and preferences often tie directly into the school size. If your child seems excited about a participatory environment, I would look for smaller schools, with a low student-to-teacher ratio. Some students learn best in small, intimate class settings. They have a better opportunity to interact with professors and contribute to the learning environment. Other students, however, learn better in lecture-style classrooms by taking notes and listening to a professor.

Social and extracurricular factors play a part in the size conversation as well. Very social teenagers might want a larger school with more social options, clubs, and teams. If this is the case with your child, in addition to a medium-to-large school, you might look for an active on-campus scene and an involved office of student events. Likewise, look at the number of students who commute to campus. A small school with a large percentage of commuters usually implies a less-active campus community. If campus activity is less important for your child, you don't need to prioritize schools based on the answer to this question.

Ask your child to consider these questions if he is unsure:

- Do you want to be at a college that is smaller or larger than your high school?
- Do you want to know most of your classmates or feel a bit anonymous?
- In general, do you want to be in large lecture halls for class or small classrooms with fewer students?
- Is it important to go to a school with a nationally known sports team?
- My size preference is:_____.
- On a scale of 1 to 10, how important is a school's size to your decision?_____

Type of School

Colleges and universities fall into a variety of categories based on their academic course offerings. These are the major categories of schools.

- **Liberal Arts Colleges.** Liberal arts colleges help students refine written, verbal, and analytical skills while receiving a broad-based education. Liberal arts colleges are generally small-to-medium-sized. Examples: Colby College, Washington and Lee University, Lafayette College, Colorado College, Muhlenberg College.
- **Specialty Schools.** Specialty schools are for students who have a clear academic/career direction and want a school that focuses on that passion. Examples: Babson College (business), Rhode Island School of Design (arts), Juilliard (performing arts).

- **National Universities.** National universities can provide students both liberal arts and specialty options. They are generally (but not always) medium- to large-sized and offer a number of different preprofessional options for students, such as communications, physical therapy, or business majors. Examples: Cornell University, Carnegie Mellon University, University of Virginia, University of Pennsylvania, Syracuse University, Boston College.

This issue relates back to school and class size. Large, national universities have larger class enrollment and subsequently, lend themselves to lecture-style classes. Small liberal arts colleges tend to have more informal class structures, encouraging interaction with professors and peers.

Note that liberal arts schools may require students to take 50 percent of their classes from a core curriculum. If your child is hoping to explore many interests during college, you should look into schools with less structured requirements, such as national universities.

Specialty schools often have multiple course requirements, mostly because enrolled students attend specific programs in the specialty area (e.g., culinary arts or interior design).

There are a few other "types" of colleges that are subcategories of the types listed above. These include women's colleges, such as Smith, Mount Holyoke, or Barnard; traditionally African-American colleges, such as Morehouse or Spelman; and religiously affiliated schools, such as College of the Holy Cross, Yeshiva University, or Fairfield University.

Here are some specific questions to guide your discussion of this potential list driver:

- Is there course work you definitely want to experience while in college (for example, accounting, electrical engineering, or fashion design)?
- If appropriate, would you like to consider colleges where everyone is of your gender, ethnicity, or religion?

- My school type preference is: _____.
- On a scale of 1 to 10, how important is school type to your decision? _____

If your child's goals are mainly career related, you may also want to consider the career services office and research the number, type, and quality of companies that recruit students on campus for employment after graduation. A specialty business school or national university may have many contacts in large cities and invite notable corporations to recruit on campus. Liberal arts schools can certainly prepare students for many careers, so do not rule these out if your child has specific career goals. However, if your child's top priority is to get a business job after graduation, you may want to emphasize schools with strong economics departments or even graduate business programs that open classes to juniors and seniors. Many liberal arts school graduates certainly go on to excellent professional careers, but liberal arts schools also tend to send a higher percentage of students on to graduate school. This is not a negative; it's just something to think about. If school type turns out to be one of your child's list drivers, then it's worthwhile to look at job search support at the schools you are considering for your list.

Major

The previous section on school type leads into a discussion of a potential major. For instance, if your son eats, sleeps, and drinks news, he may want to major in journalism and have this be a top college list driver. In that case, he should not apply to a school that does not offer a journalism major.

Many students are undecided about a major, and that is fine. But for those teenagers who are clear about their course of study, this can be an important list driver. These days, about 50 percent of the students apply to college without a strong inclination of what they should major in, while 50 percent of students say they know their plans. If your child has a very strong interest in a particular area, then this will likely be an important list driver for you.

Here are some questions to guide your child:

- Do you have a major (or a few possibilities) in mind?
- Do you want to attend a school with a wide variety of major choices because you are undecided?
- What are your current feelings about graduate school or a future career? (If student is very clear on future goals, he might prioritize that issue as a list driver for college selection.)
- Do you think any of your hobbies or extracurricular interests might be something you would like to pursue as a career? For instance, if your daughter is an excellent musician, she may want to attend a school that offers a music major and not just a school with good music clubs or activities.
- The major I would like to look for in a college is: _____.
- On a scale of 1 to 10, how important is major to your decision? _____

If your student has a specific major in mind, you should make sure each college offers the program.

Learning Services

Is it typical for your child to need extra help from a teacher outside of class or the services of a tutor? Do you believe this will continue to be the case in college? All colleges attempt to accommodate students with different learning styles, but some do it better than others.

Remember that sometimes the academic needs of a student will trump all other college preferences. If this is the case in your family, look at the services for each school, whether it's availability of professors, class lectures on tape, a twenty-four-hour tutoring center, or joint library privileges among local colleges, and make this your most important list driver.

- On a scale of 1 to 10, how important are academic services to your decision? (Note: If this is essential, you must rank it a 10). _____

Sports

Does your student want to play a sport in college? Sports can be a large part of a student's social life. Not every college offers every sport, so be sure to research availability. Before making sports a list driver, though, talk to your child's coach to assess his realistic chances for playing his sport in college and determining what division is appropriate. Also, if a high school star soccer player doesn't want the pressure of competitive college sports, determine which schools have vital intramural programs. If your child is a candidate for varsity sports at a college, you have likely heard from your child's coach already. If your child is not top tier but enjoys athletics, sports can still be an important consideration. Here are some guidelines:

- Do you have an interest in participating in a sport? If so, which one, what division, and are intramural sports an acceptable alternative?
- Have coaches verified the level at which you might realistically play?
- The sport I would like to play is: _____.
- The level of sport I would like to participate in is: _____.
- On a scale of 1 to 10, how important is sports (or a particular sport) to your decision?_____

Clubs and Cultural Activities

Clearly your child's high school activities list can help guide the decision of what types of extracurricular activities he will look for in a college. But your child may also want to try something completely new. When discussing what activities your child might want to pursue, do your best to determine what activities are "must haves" and which are "nice-to-haves." Here are some questions to guide you:

- Are there any clubs, activities, or cultural opportunities (e.g., exposure to museums, theater, art exhibits, and concerts) that you must have in a college? *List them here:*

_____ _____
_____ _____
_____ _____
_____ _____

- On a scale of 1 to 10, how important is it for a college to have each of the activities you listed?

Fraternity/Sorority

Is your child currently involved in social clubs or organizations, including spirit clubs, student activities committees, or religious youth organizations? These may be an indication that your child would want to participate in Greek life on a college campus. Most kids have a sense if this is the right choice for them. It can often be an important driver for certain students who are particularly social, or whose parents or older siblings participated in a fraternity or sorority. When assessing schools, you can look into the number of students who participate in Greek life on campus. Some colleges have up to 90 percent Greek life participation. Of course, a child who dislikes fraternities might feel excluded in that college environment. If this is the case for your child, then "No Greek life" may be a list driver.

- Do you prefer a school with no Greek life, some Greek life, or a strong Greek life?
- Are you interested in the professional networking opportunities a fraternity or sorority network might provide in the future?
- On a scale of 1 to 10, how important is this factor to your decision? _____

Cost

Cost can be a driver for some families; if it is an important issue for your family, it needs to be considered early in the admissions process. I recommend that students with financial need apply to schools regardless of cost and then apply for financial aid. Don't assume that you won't get the money you need if your family cannot afford to pay for college.

However, if cost is a driver for you, then you might want to consider having your child apply to a "financial safety school," where you could afford the cost even without financial aid, such as your local state school. You can also consider schools where your child might have a better chance of receiving a recruitment scholarship. For much more on this topic and how to incorporate it into your college search, see chapter 10.

• Note if cost is a driver in your decision: _____

X Factors

Every student is different, and some have unique preferences or needs that we haven't covered so far. If your child has a specific course, activity, or location he wants to find in a college, then by all means use that as a criteria. I have seen a young woman who needed to attend a college where she could have a stable for her horse. I have seen a young man who wanted to join a poetry writing club and only applied to schools with that possibility. In these cases, the families did their own Internet and library research to find schools that matched their child's precise need.

Some other "x factors" might be: independent study, study abroad programs, student-designed majors, work-study programs, or teacher certification programs.

• List any "x factor" that you must have at the college you attend:

_____

II. TURNING PREFERENCES INTO LIST DRIVERS

Now that you have answered all of the above questions with your child, it's time to put the results together to determine the list drivers you will apply to the college selection process. In this section you will translate your child's answers into criteria that you can use to narrow down schools.

Everyone has preferences, but you can't use all of your preferences to narrow down school lists. Your goal should be determining your child's *must haves* versus his *nice-to-haves*. Go back over your child's answers and list all of the factors in priority order to determine which factors are most important. Remember, if your child requires tutoring for a learning disability or has another academic or physical need, then those factors must be considered in the top three list drivers. If a particular factor was not important at all, feel free to leave it off the chart entirely. The top three ranked factors will serve as your major list drivers in the college search. Here is an example for a student named Adam:

Scale of Importance	Factor	Preference
10	Major	Would like to major in business —not economics
10	Type of school	Very career-oriented, wants a specialty or national university
9	Geography	New England or Mid-Atlantic, but no farther
8	*Competitiveness*	*The more competitive, the better*
7	*Sports*	*Intramural tennis would be nice, but not required*
7	*Academic services*	*Would benefit from easy access to tutoring, but not required*
6	*Fraternities*	*A plus, but not required*

So, Adam should let geography, major and type of school drive his college list. In addition, it would be "nice to have" some of the other criteria as well, but it would be unwise to eliminate schools based upon those criteria.

Now complete this exercise for your child:

Scale of Importance	Factor	Preference

WARNING!

At the beginning of the college selection process students may not be completely honest or certain about their priorities. For instance, a student will not be sure (or may not admit) that Division III football is a priority and he will apply to some schools that don't have the sport. Instead he will say, "Let's just see where I get in." If this same boy later decides that football is a priority, he will face a tough choice if some of the schools that accept him don't have a football program. In some instances, it is only a student's safety school that has football.

To avoid facing this dilemma in your family, work with your child *now* to talk through priorities. This is incredibly important.

Narrow the List by Your Child's List Drivers

The first "culling" of your college list should be a quick college database search on the Web. Now that your child knows what he wants and you've assessed how competitive he really is as an applicant, there are hundreds of free matching tools on the Web that can help narrow a list of schools using the exact criteria. Web site search tools will ask for your criteria, such as location, major, size, campus life, and selectivity, and then the search engines find the schools that offer the features you are searching for. You can also visit your local bookstore or library to skim through one of the many college guides available for parents and students.

Here are a few specific Web sites that you may want to use to find information, database searches, or book recommendations:

www.petersons.com
www.collegeboard.com
www.princetonreview.com

These sites may help to confirm or change your thoughts about a particular college or university that your child is considering. For our student example above, I did a database search using only his three list drivers of geography, major, and type of school as search criteria. The criteria narrowed down the college list to approximately two hundred schools. Please know that I believe the database, in isolation, is a pretty insignificant piece of the college selection process. That being said, the database still plays a role at the beginning of the narrowing process.

In addition to database searches, parents and children will spend hours surfing the Web, looking at college Web sites, hoping the images are of a campus they may visit or even attend. The Internet is a wonderful resource to provide insight regarding future opportunities or even a virtual campus tour. When you do visit college Web sites that look appealing, you should request information via mail. This way you can get on the mailing list to receive updates about each school.

III. DETERMINE THE STRENGTH OF YOUR CHILD'S CANDIDACY

Your child's list drivers and his standing as an overall candidate will help him build a list and eliminate inappropriate schools. The critical component of college selection is the careful thinking about the student's criteria as well as a comprehensive and accurate understanding of his qualifications. Ultimately, you will narrow your choices down to seven schools—two Dream schools, three Just Right schools, and two No Problem schools—where your child will send applications. Frequently, students apply to an unreasonable number of schools and are consequently bombarded with too much work—thus, the final product suffers. Therefore, this 2:3:2 ratio provides a manageable amount of work, yet still yields a strong number of acceptances. If you take the process step-by-step, you will be able to narrow down your child's list from two hundred schools to seven—I promise!

The next critical step is to realistically assess where your child stands academically among his peers. How strong of an applicant is he really? By taking stock, you can avoid your child getting his hopes up about a school where he has no real chance of admission.

Step 1. Look at your child's overall candidacy: grades, test scores, and "the rest"

The best way to determine the strength of a student's candidacy is by reviewing *everything* that he would send to the colleges on his list. You will want to look at your child's grades and course difficulty—is he taking Advanced Placement, honors, college preparatory, or something else? Grades, course difficulty, and rank should be lumped into one category; they are the primary area that a college will review.

Secondary to the transcript are the standardized tests: SAT I and SAT II or ACT. What are your child's best scores?

The third critical piece is what we like to call "the rest." "The rest" includes the extracurricular activities, essays, letters of recommendation, and interviews—and of course, how well these are described on applications. Each of these areas can strongly influence an admissions decision, as you will learn in the next several chapters of this book. It is important to pay attention to every component of the application process, no matter how strong your child's grades and test scores might be. For now, compare your child's extracurricular achievements to those of his classmates: is your child's extracurricular profile stronger, weaker, or about the same as other kids in the class? We will apply this information in the chart below.

Step 2. Research average GPA and test scores at the schools on your child's list

The next step is to compare your child's cumulative high school GPA and SAT or ACT scores against the freshman average for a school your child is considering. These scores are usually found in any college guidebook, university Web site, or by contacting the college admissions office. (Note that GPAs can be tricky because some schools publish "weighted" GPAs and some use "unweighted." When in doubt about GPAs, match your child's SAT score and his grades with those listed in the table below.) By considering these numbers, you will get a better sense for a college's selectivity. This also narrows down your school choices, simply by eliminating colleges that are not a good academic fit.

Step 3. Assess where your child fits on the selectivity scale

How can you determine where your child fits on the selectivity scale? Based on your student's grades and SAT scores, choose from the selectivity categories in Chart 1 below to decide which area *best* describes your child's academic profile. This will be the selectivity level of your child's "Just Right" category.

Notes on This Chart

If applicable, to convert ACT scores to SAT scores use Chart 2. Since most students do not fit neatly into a category, the tiebreaker becomes "the rest" mentioned above. If your child is between categories (for instance, a B student with a 1350 SAT score), assess his extracurricular profile compared to other students at his school with similar grades and/or SAT scores. Note: no student should move up or down more than one category. So if you think his extracurricular profile is stronger than average (e.g., leadership positions, varsity sports, extensive community service), then you can also circle the B+/1300 category. If you think his extracurricular profile is weaker than average, then circle the B/1200 category.

Chart 1: Where Does Your Child Fall on the College Selectivity Scale?

Selectivity Category	GPA is closest to . . .	SAT score is closest to . . .	Difficulty of most classes is . . .
A 1500	A	1500	AP Schedule
A- 1400	A-	1400	AP/Honors Schedule
B+ 1300	B+	1300	Honors Schedule
B 1200	B	1200	Honors Schedule
B- 1100	B-	1100	College Prep schedule
C+ 1000	C+	1000	College Prep Schedule
C 900	C	900	College Prep Schedule
Below C	C- or lower	900 or lower	Fulfills High School Graduation Requirements

Chart 2 (if necessary)
How to Convert an ACT Score to an SAT
Score to Complete the Above Chart

ACT Composite Score	SAT I Score (Verbal and Math)
36	1600
35	1580
34	1520
33	1470
32	1420
31	1380
30	1340
29	1300
28	1260
27	1220
26	1180
25	1140
24	1110
23	1070
22	1030
21	990
20	950
19	910
18	870
17	830
16	780
15	740
14	680
13	620
12	560
11	500

Let's go back to our example of Adam. He had a B+ average, 1250 on his SAT, and an impressive list of activities, including class president, captain of the tennis team, president of a religious youth organization, and a year-round volunteer tennis teacher. From academics alone, it appears that he would fall in between categories B+/1300 and B/1200. Although he consistently achieves a B+ average in course work, he did not score a 1300 on the SAT. However, because he has a very strong activities résumé, Adam can safely categorize B+/1300 schools into his Just Right category, even though his actual scores were slightly lower. It is important to know that "the rest" can move your child's Just Right designation up a full category on the scale. Conversely, an academically strong student, without a good activities résumé, can move down a category on the scale.

Step 4. Decide your criteria for Dream, Just Right, and No Problem categories

Now that your child's Just Right selectivity category is set, your child can consider applying to schools that are one category above the Just Right category, his Dream level of schools. Note that you should always eliminate schools more than one category above since the likelihood of admission is extremely low.

To determine No Problem schools, consider applying to schools one or two levels below the Just Right category. You should not apply to any schools three or more categories below your "Just Right" level, since those schools will not be academically challenging.

Let's return to our original example of Adam. Adam's Just Right schools were those in the B+/1300 scale. Therefore, applying the "one above, two below" rule, he can also apply to schools in the A-/1400 range, as well as schools in the B/1200 and B-/1100 category. He should immediately eliminate schools in the A/1500 range or schools at C+/1000 level or below.

Other elements to consider at this point are the "nice-to-have" factors your child mentioned in the exercises in the first section of this chapter. These factors, if they are present at many of the schools that also feature your child's list drivers and fit with his academic standing, can tip the scales in favor of one school over another with a similar profile.

WARNING! BE CAREFUL WHEN ASSESSING THE AVERAGE SAT SCORES OF COLLEGES

Once you know your child's top composite SAT score, how do you determine where it fits at a given college? Colleges publish their average range of SAT scores, called "the middle 50th percentile." This range represents the middle 50 percent of applicants, which means that 25 percent of applicants have SAT scores above the high end of the range and 25 percent are below the low end of the range. Students will often look at the range and mistakenly think that because their scores fall within the range, they should not have a problem gaining admission. However, *where* the student's scores fall within the range is very important. Being in the middle to high end of the published range usually reflects a better chance of admission than if the student is in the lowest quarter of the range.

The Dream schools, also known as "reach schools," are those where your child's GPA and SAT scores are below the average numbers published by that particular institution. For Dream schools, there is less than a 50 percent chance he will be admitted. Remember, however, that "dream" is a relative term that applies to your child with his individual profile, wants, and needs. Everyone's dream is not an Ivy League school. Be realistic.

The Just Right, or midrange schools, are the colleges where your child's GPA and SAT scores are almost identical. In other words, your child's selectivity category matches the exact range of SAT scores and GPA the college publishes. These are usually the schools that seem to be a perfect fit academically. At this type of school, there is a greater than 50 percent chance that your child will be admitted.

No Problem schools, or "safeties," are those schools in which your child's GPA and SAT scores are higher than the average published scores. He will have a greater than 90 percent chance of being admitted to that institution.

NEW RULE OF COLLEGE ADMISSIONS: SCHOOLS THAT MAY SURPRISE YOU

As you work with your child to find schools to match his criteria and the right selectivity category, note that schools can change over the years. Schools can jump from the C+/1000 category to the B-/1100 or B/1200 category and become a lot more challenging to get into. This is why it is important to do your research.

For example, here are some schools that have become significantly more selective in the past ten years:

- College of New Jersey
- Northeastern University
- University of Delaware
- University of Maryland

During your database searches, keep your eyes peeled for other schools that may surprise you.

Step 5. Match schools to your child's criteria

At this point, you can work with your child to match real schools to his real chances of being admitted. Return to the Internet databases and other research you conducted to find schools that matched your child's list drivers. By this point, your child will likely have some favorites and will be able to eliminate several schools that are no longer realistic given his grades, test scores, and the rest. Use this space below to list all of the schools your child likes in each category that fit, based on their average GPAs and SAT scores. In the next section, we will ensure a balanced list of final schools to which your child will apply.

List the schools that fit your child's Just Right category based on your child's selectivity category profile from Chart 1:

_____
_____
_____

List the schools that fit your child's Dream category:

_____
_____
_____

List the schools that fit your child's No Problem category:

_____
_____
_____

IV. CREATE A 2:3:2 RATIO

Once you have divided schools into one of the three categories, you and your child should narrow the list down further, to reach a manageable number of applications. This round of eliminations can be determined by anything—your visit, the brochure, information sessions, on-campus housing, et cetera. There is, however, a ratio that should be taken into consideration when deciding how many schools your child should apply to:

- 2 Dream schools
- 3 Just Right schools
- 2 No Problem schools

If your student really wants to apply to more Dream schools, make sure he adds another school to each of the other two categories, to maintain a balanced ratio. Based on my experience, seven really is the ideal number of schools so your child can focus and compile the best applications possible. Completing fewer than five applications is too risky, in my opinion. And if students are completing more than ten applications, they are usually spreading themselves too thin. As long as a student has a good range of schools, do not worry about applying to more than seven schools.

Let's go back to Adam. If you remember, after listing his criteria for a college, he came up with 200 matches. Then, he added the selectivity rating, and determined his Just Right schools were in the 1300 SAT range. After looking at each category, completing additional research and using the 2:3:2 ratio, he ultimately applied to:

- Dream: Boston College and New York University
- Just Right: Babson College, University of Maryland, and Boston University
- No Problem: University of Vermont and Northeastern University

Use this space to record your child's 2:3:2 selections:

Category	School
Dream 1	
Dream 2	
Just Right 1	
Just Right 2	
Just Right 3	
No Problem 1	
No Problem 2	

Occasionally, you will hear stories about students who were not accepted to any of the schools to which they applied. This is usually because families have not been honest about their child's academic and extracurricular profile. Also, there are no guarantees that a child who is right in the middle 50 percent of the average GPA and SAT scores will be admitted.

What becomes more challenging is that your child will be naturally drawn to Dream schools. Although the chances of acceptance are smaller, he should still apply to these schools if they truly are only one category above his Just Rights. Sometimes, dreams do come true. It is extremely important that your child apply to schools in each of the selectivity categories to ensure he has options once the decision letters arrive. The ultimate goal is to ensure that wherever your child is admitted, he will feel good about the outcome and have all of his academic and social needs fulfilled.

WARNING! DON'T BE TOP-HEAVY

One of the most common mistakes I see in the college selection process occurs when families are top-heavy in their lists. They throw in some "Hail Mary" applications to schools that are beyond Dreams, just to see what happens. This is really a waste of time and can be demoralizing for a child who gets his hopes up. In reality, it's best to be middle-heavy, hence the 2:3:2 ratio, so that your child has more options rather than fewer when decision letters start to arrive.

Remember, too, that Just Right schools are certainly not guaranteed acceptances. Unfortunately, there are no guarantees in the college admissions process, so our goal is to help you to be realistic, hedge your bets, and create the very best outcome based on your child's academics, test scores, and extracurricular record.

As you have learned, it is crucial to spend time and effort determining your child's list drivers and competitiveness for maximum happiness and academic challenge. The more honest your child is during the process, the more happy and fulfilled he is likely to feel once he arrives on campus.

CHAPTER 4

THE APPLICATION

Expert Coach: Heather Beveridge,
Former Admissions Officer, New York University

Now that you and your child have narrowed down the list, your next step is to gather the applications together. But with seven schools, seven sets of forms, and countless essays, the paperwork can quickly feel overwhelming. Many parents and students tell me that the process of completing multiple college applications is far more stressful than awaiting admissions decisions. But there is a strategy that can make things a whole lot easier: organization.

When students and families have an organized approach to applications, essays, interviews, and deadlines, they regain a sense of control over a process that often seems unpredictable and unmanageable. Creating an organizational system that keeps you informed of requirements and one step ahead of deadlines leads to less stress and more success.

RULES TO REMEMBER IN THIS CHAPTER

- **A little organization goes a long way.** Organize yourself early in the process to minimize stress over your child's responsibilities, deadlines, scheduling visits, and more.

- **Early application options are just that—options.** Understand the myriad application options available and the benefits and drawbacks of each. Then you can make an informed decision about which application options are appropriate for your child.
- **Understand the application.** Most college applications are made up of four sections: Personal Information, Activity Chart, Short Essay, and Personal Statement/Major Essay. Breaking down a college application into its four key sections allows for organized and successful completion. Using the Common Application, when schools offer this option, can make the application process even smoother.
- **Know your high school's role in the process.** Each high school guidance office takes a different approach to assisting its students with compiling their application materials. Understand the procedures and deadlines at your child's high school to develop the best possible working relationship with the guidance office—and to avoid any mistakes or missed deadlines.
- **Set your child up for success.** Share organizational tips, advice, and good work habits with your child throughout the application writing and submission process. This will lessen your stress as a parent and result in a positive experience for your child.

I. SEVEN STEPS TO APPLICATION ORGANIZATION

Step 1. Make a plan with your child

The perfect time for you to establish an application plan with your child is while reviewing and organizing what needs to be done to complete the applications. I often field questions from parents about how much they should do to help their child complete the applications. They are torn between wanting their child to take the initiative and responsibility to complete the applications herself and wanting to help in any way they can. Often they feel that their son or daughter isn't focusing on getting the applications completed, and they are worried applications might be late, riddled with mistakes, or both.

Part of getting organized involves talking to your child about a timeline for completing applications, who will proofread them, and who is responsible for making sure they are sent on time. By having a discussion with your child about your expectations early in the process, each of you will be aware of the other's role. I recommend sitting down with your calendar and your child's calendar at the beginning of the application process—perhaps on a quiet weekend afternoon—to map out time for everything that needs to get done, including brainstorming essays, writing essays, revising essays, setting up interviews, and all test and application deadlines.

As much as you would like to help, your child is the one applying to college. He needs to be the one to complete the forms, ask for recommendations, and write the essays. However, at some point you will probably find yourself checking to see if test scores were sent, reminding him that the first application is due in four days, and checking the calendar to make sure the application is submitted by the deadline.

Clearly communicate to your child what level of involvement you expect to have and what his responsibilities are *before* he begins working on applications. You should discuss:

- An overall schedule for completing college applications. This is why it is so important to coordinate calendars and write down everything. Make sure you consider family commitments, athletic and extracurricular schedules, any deadlines from your child's high school, and remember to allow time for the unexpected. For example, if your family has a very full schedule in December because of the holidays, and your child has a Model United Nations conference, four performances with the school chorus, and starts practices for a winter sport at the same time, then you might want to set December 1 as the goal for completing applications.

- Your child should have someone take a look at his applications before he submits them. This can be a friend, teacher, counselor, sibling, or you. It should be someone who knows the student well and someone from whom he will take constructive criticism. If your child is comfortable having you read his applications, don't be afraid to point out clear mistakes or make suggestions about essays or short answers. After all, you've known your child longer than anyone else; but in the end, it must be his work. If your child is uncomfortable with you reading his essays, ask if you can review the rest of the application but suggest that a teacher or family friend read the essays.
- Schedule some time when you are *not* going to talk about college applications. As much time as you might spend thinking about your child applying to college, she is thinking about it more. Consider how many times you have heard neighbors, relatives, or classmates ask your child about college. As important as the college application process may seem, there are a lot of other things going on in her life. Remember to take time for talking about other things.

Step 2. Make a master chart
Once your child has a final list of schools that he will apply to, chart all of the application requirements for each school. You can do this on a spreadsheet or on note cards—find a system that works best for your family. Your chart should include the following elements: school name, address, telephone number, Web site, application deadline(s), standardized test requirements, number of recommendations required, interview availability, application fee, Common Application acceptance and any supplements, and submission options (online/mail).

Step 3. Create individual folders
Your child should create a folder for each school, including the application for that school and any required supplemental information that school requires. For many schools, the file will contain a copy of the Common Application (described in detail later

in this chapter). Keep copies of everything you send, including a printout of anything submitted online, and write down any confirmation numbers, user names, and passwords.

Step 4. Develop an essay inventory

An essay inventory is a composite list of all essay questions required across all schools that your child is applying to. This tool will allow your student to understand the overlaps between schools as well as assess their overall essay workload. (For more on this topic, see chapter 6.)

Step 5. Plan recommendations

Have your child start thinking about which teachers he would like to write his recommendations. He should have two teachers in mind, in addition to his guidance counselor. (See chapter 8.)

Step 6. Schedule visits, interviews, and auditions

Keep in mind that many schools may not offer interviews, but if they do, they may offer not only on-campus but also local alumni options for interviews. (See chapter 9.)

Step 7. Get started!

As you will see below, schools offer various timelines for admissions decisions, so it pays to start the process as early as possible.

II. WHEN TO APPLY: ROLLING, REGULAR, AND EARLY OPTIONS

While each college can set its own application deadlines, there are some general options and timelines that I'll address in this section. Applications are updated each year, and the new applications are typically available during the summer leading up to senior year. In particular, the Common Application is updated and typically made available on July 1. If your child wants to work on applications over the summer, make certain he isn't using last year's application.

Colleges will usually have either fixed application deadlines and notification dates, or they will operate on a "rolling admissions" plan. Here is an outline of the various application options and how to determine which is best for your child.

Rolling Admissions

Rolling admissions is most common at public universities. Under a rolling admissions plan, complete applications are reviewed once they are submitted, and decisions are sent out as they are reached. If your child is applying to a school with rolling admissions, he should apply as early as possible. Competition for spaces increases later in the school year. For example, a student has a better chance of getting accepted when there are still 90 percent of the spots open. That same student may not look quite as strong if his application is reviewed when 90 percent of the class has been selected.

The bottom line: get the application in early to maximize chances of admission. There is no downside to applying as early as possible to a school with rolling admissions.

Regular Decision

Colleges and universities with fixed deadlines and notification dates may have more than one admissions plan. All schools with fixed deadlines will offer what is known as regular decision. Under regular decision, most application deadlines occur between January 1 and February 1, although some may be as early as December or as late as March. Students who apply through regular decision will receive a response from the college on or around April 1. The student generally has until May 1 to make his decision on where to attend and commit to a college.

Early Decision and Early Action

Many schools also offer an early decision or early action option. Under early decision or early action, students apply by an earlier date, usually November 1 to December 1, but maybe as early as

October or as late as February. A student can expect a response under early decision or early action anywhere from one to two months after the deadline. A common example for the early timeline is a November 1 application deadline and a December 15 notification date. There is, however, a major difference between early decision and early action.

Early Decision

Under early decision, a student agrees that if he is offered admission to the college, he will withdraw any other applications and attend that college. Thus, once an early decision student is admitted, he is finished with the entire application process, since the early decision agreement commits the student to attend that college.

In general, I believe students have a slight admissions advantage by applying early decision, because colleges want to lock in a part of their freshman class early and boost the percentage of students accepting their offers of admission (their "yield"). Beyond that, colleges are like people. If you tell people they are your favorite or your first choice, it usually prompts them to look at you in a more positive light. Early decision lets colleges know a certain portion of the freshman class genuinely wanted to be at their school more than at any other, and they argue those enthusiastic students make a difference on their campus.

Early Action

Early action acceptances are *not* binding. Early action students who are admitted may choose to be done with their application process at that time, or may choose to wait for decisions on other applications and make their choice on where to attend by May 1. This flexibility exists because early action is just what it implies: a chance to act early. Overall, unlike early decision which provides an admissions advantage—early action is typically an admissions-neutral option. In contrast to early decision, this option does not guarantee the college a certain percentage of enrolled students. For the college, there are limited advantages to admitting a student early action versus regular decision.

Even though there may be no admissions advantage to applying early action, it is nice to get a "yes" under your belt early in
the admissions cycle.

The Benefits and Pitfalls of Early Programs

I often find myself speaking with students and parents who have
decided that they "must" apply early. While I do believe that early
decision and early action can be good options for some students,
they certainly are not the right choice for every student.

For a young woman who does have a clear first choice—a college she knows she would attend no matter what the other schools
on her list offered and knows it will still be her first choice a year
from now—an early decision application allows that student to increase her chances of acceptance and learn the admissions decision
(and, we hope, finish this process) a few months early.

What if your child doesn't have a first-choice college as the
early deadlines approach? First, know that it is okay. Despite what
you hear from other parents, what might happen in your child's
school, or what is discussed in the media, most students do not
apply early. Think of how your child has changed over the past six
months, or year, and how much he might change between now
and the start of his freshman year in college. It might be too early
to make a decision that commits him to attend a particular college. He might have three schools that he likes equally, but for
different reasons. Or maybe he hasn't had a chance to visit all of
the schools in which he is interested. If this is the case, early decision is not a good idea. If a college offers an early action program,
he may still wish to apply early. He will still be able to hear from
other schools and take the time to think through his decision.

Another common concern about early programs is financial
aid or scholarships. Paying for college is a major commitment for
any student and any family. If financial aid or scholarships will be
a determining factor in where your child will attend college, early
decision is not the best option. Early decision applicants will be
considered for financial aid and scholarships just like other students and will receive an estimate of need-based financial aid and

perhaps merit-based scholarships when they find out they have been admitted. However, at that point you will only have your early decision school's offer and will not be able to sit down and compare offers from different colleges. This is not the case with early action, as students have until May 1 to respond. This allows them to hear from other colleges and compare their financial aid packages or scholarship offers.

You should also consider whether your child would have a stronger application if he waited until January to apply. This is particularly true for students whose grades are on a strong upward trend or who had a recent term or semester where the grades were not up to their usual level. Suppose a student has a slow start in high school. His grades in ninth and the first part of tenth grade are average, but something happens near the end of sophomore year and he begins to take off academically. The trend continues in junior year, he earns his best grades ever and is promoted to honors courses for senior year. This student might benefit from waiting for regular decision where he can show the admissions officers his academic performance has continued to improve in more difficult classes.

Lastly, it is possible that a child who applies early will be denied admission. Will your child be able to take that decision in stride or will it affect the rest of his senior year? Hearing that your favorite college cannot offer you admission is hard enough at any time. However, getting that news in isolation is different than getting it when you also have a few offers of admissions in hand. You don't want your child to feel demoralized, so discuss the emotional consequences as openly as you can and take into consideration your child's sensitivity.

DON'T PANIC! DEALING WITH EARLY REJECTIONS AND DEFERRALS

Keep in mind that students may also be denied admission under an early decision or early action plan. If a student is denied admission under an early decision plan, he may not reapply to the same school as a regular decision candidate. It is discouraging to get rejected from a school through an early option, but this is also very good information. If what you thought was a No Problem school rejects your child, this is a strong indication that you need to revise your list.

An early application may also be deferred to regular decision and considered with the rest of the applicant pool. This is often the case when the college wants the opportunity to compare this individual with the entire applicant pool or wants to see senior year grades before making a decision. If your child is deferred through an early program, it is often a good idea to send updated information as it becomes available to augment and strengthen the application. He will also be required to send an updated transcript that includes midyear grades.

To review, here is a chart to help your decision making.

Admission Plan	*Always* apply under this plan if . . .	*Never* apply under this plan if . . .
Early Decision	1. You have a clear first-choice school and do not mind committing no matter what. 2. Financial concerns will not be a factor in deciding on a college.	1. You are not 100 percent certain that you want to go to this school. 2. Financial aid considerations matter. 3. Your grades, activities, and test scores are on a significant upward trend. 4. Rejection would be personally devastating.
Early Action	1. You are confident that your application is going to be just as strong early senior year as later. This includes grades, activities, and test scores.	1. Your grades, activities, and test scores are on a significant upward trend. 2. You do not have enough time to put together a quality application.

III. GETTING TO KNOW THE COLLEGE APPLICATION

No matter what admissions option(s) you choose with your child, the application will look the same. The four key sections include: Personal Information and Academic Background, Activity Chart, Short Essay, and Personal Statement/Major Essay. Here is an overview of each section of the application and some insight into what admissions officers will be looking for.

Personal Information

A college application starts with the basics, such as name, date of birth, address, and so on. The personal data section is usually the first segment of the application. The college might even have a separate form that asks for most or all of this information and requests that you return it (along with the application fee) earlier than the remainder of the application. The application may also request optional information, such as place of birth, first or native language, religious affiliation, race or ethnicity, and family information.

Understanding the Context

The personal data section of the application asks many questions that at first glance seem irrelevant. Why do the colleges ask for all of this information? Obviously they need to know how to contact the applicant. They also need to know if he is applying as a freshman or a transfer or applying to a specific program or major, but why are they interested in where a parent or sibling went to college? Does a student's ethnicity, religion, native language, or if they have siblings matter in this process?

When reviewing an application, admissions officers are going to consider academics, activities, essays, and recommendations. They may take interviews, auditions, portfolios, or athletic ability into consideration, if they are applicable. But they also want to review all of this information in the proper context. Many of these questions are on the application to get the necessary background information.

For example, a student's transcript might reveal that he struggled with English in his freshman year, showed steady improvement in sophomore year, did very well in junior year, and moved into an honors course for senior year. Any admissions officer would be interested in that upward trend in a major academic subject, but isn't it helpful to know facts such as the student's first language was not English, English is not the primary language used at home, and neither parent attended college in the United States?

Another student has a stellar academic record in her freshman and junior years. In her sophomore year, the first quarter is strong. The second and third marking periods show a dramatic drop in her grades and the fourth quarter has a slight improvement. If you were an admissions officer reviewing her file, would you want to know that her parents separated in the fall of her sophomore year? There are questions on the Common Application and most other applications that ask about divorce, even asking for the date in many cases. If divorce or other family situation has had a negative effect on your child, it is also helpful if the guidance counselor mentions it. Sometimes there is a section on the application giving the student an opportunity to provide any additional information such as this, but, as you've seen in previous chapters, it is always better to have someone else tell your story so it sounds less like an excuse. However, if you feel you have no other options, use the application to explain what happened.

For an admissions officer, knowing the circumstances that surround a student's academic and extracurricular record may make a difference. Each question on its own may not provide exceptionally useful information for every student. However, knowing the information can help admissions officers develop a more complete picture of each applicant's academic, extracurricular, and personal accomplishments.

Some colleges or programs within universities also may have a specific mission that is reflected in its optional application questions. For instance, state colleges and universities may limit the number of students from outside their home state because their primary mission is to educate state residents. A religiously affiliated college may give preference to students of the same faith. A university might have a program that seeks to encourage more women to major in engineering. Another school may have a desire to promote higher education for students whose parents did not attend college. Yet another may seek to enroll students from groups traditionally underrepresented on their campus. Colleges may also give special consideration to students who have a parent or sibling who attended the college. That explains some of the questions. But why might they want to know a student's ethnic group, religion, or the occupations of their parents? Is it truly necessary to answer the "optional" questions?

The answer is a resounding yes. While colleges and universities are seeking to build a dynamic learning community, they are also seeking to build a strong community outside of the classroom. They also need the college community to fulfill the mission of the individual school. By answering the optional questions, you are helping the admissions committee understand you better, thus adding to the diversity of their student body. Remember that diversity relates not only to ethnicity, but also to socioeconomic class, type of school experience (public, private, charter, home schooling), family circumstances, extracurricular interests, and more. A classroom filled with students with differing backgrounds can enrich learning opportunities for all.

I attended high school in a pretty homogenous community. For most of my life, I lived in places where the people were pretty much like me. I had some wonderful teachers, learned a lot, and thought I was well prepared for a competitive college. I still remember how much I learned in college by finding common ground with students who came from completely different backgrounds. I also found many differences with some who seemed like me at the beginning. This diversity not only was helpful to my growth as a person, it also enriched the academic experience. For example, when colonialism was discussed in a British literature class, hearing from a student whose country's emergence from colonialism was still in progress added a fresh perspective. A discussion of comparative economic systems in my macroeconomics class was much more vibrant because some of the participants had grown up in countries emerging from communism or with a strong socialist tradition and shared their own perspectives with the rest of us who knew only the system in the United States.

Sometimes the idea of diversity doesn't need to be dramatic. Just because your family didn't emigrate from another country or you only speak one language fluently doesn't mean your college community can't benefit from your contribution. For a popular East Coast school, a student from the Midwest may be more than welcome. Admissions officers want their school to represent not only a variety of ethnicities, but also a range of experiences.

College administrators and faculty know that a person's hometown, ethnic group, or socioeconomic class does not dictate her individual knowledge, beliefs, or opinions. But having a diverse student body makes it more likely that a multitude of experiences and ideas will be represented on campus, enriching the community inside and outside the classroom. The admissions office is responsible for crafting the kind of community the college desires.

Academic Background

Each application is also going to ask for information about the student's education. This section will include information such as:

- high school(s) attended and dates of attendance;
- name of guidance or college counselor;
- colleges attended or college credit earned in high school;
- what the applicant is doing if not currently in school;
- dates and results of standardized tests.

This information allows the admissions office to know which schools to expect transcripts from and whom they should contact if there are questions about the student's academic record. Is the student finished with her standardized testing or will there be new results in the coming weeks? Even when the application asks you to list the results of standardized tests, or if the scores appear on your child's transcript, still be sure to send the official score reports from the testing agency.

Activities Chart

There will be a place on the application to list extracurricular and personal activities, volunteer projects, and work experience. Most applications will provide a grid that asks students to list, in the order of importance to them, the name of the activity, years of participation and time spent on the activity, the position held or any honors won, and whether or not participation will continue in college. Even if you send an additional résumé or activity list along with the application, your child must still complete the list or grid provided in the application.

The application activities chart includes extracurriculars, volunteer work, and all other nonacademic activities. The application may also ask for any academic honors or awards the student has received, beginning in ninth grade. Your child should list any scholastic achievements and provide a short explanation of the award, if needed. Admissions officers will know what the honor roll, dean's list, or National Honors Society are but might need an explanation for something specific to your child's school. For instance, your high school or town may have its own awards for spirit, academic achievement, community service, or something else. Or your school may use acronyms to identify programs, such as RPO (Ridge Peer Organization), that are not known outside of your area. Be sure to explain briefly all activities, acronyms, and abbreviations that are not nationally recognized. This can be done briefly in the activities chart or explained as part of a short-answer essay about activities. You should also note when your child's school doesn't offer academic honors.

An admissions officer will gain insight into what to expect from a student outside of the college classroom through the applicant's record of extracurricular involvement and work experience. On a very basic level, how a young woman chooses to spend her time is an indication of what she values. The reader will also look to see how this student developed connections to fellow students and the greater community. Is this someone who will be involved in the college community and what might that involvement be?

Short Essay

There may be one or more shorter essay questions on an application. Students might be asked to write about topics such as which extracurricular activity is most important to them and why, what led them to apply to the particular college, or why they have chosen a certain field of study. While the application may ask for only a few sentences or a paragraph in response, students should remember that these short essays give them another opportunity to communicate something they feel is important to the admissions officers reading their application.

Personal Statement/Major Essay

An application will also include an opportunity for students to express their thoughts and opinions to the admissions officers in the form of an essay or personal statement. This section gives the student an opportunity to communicate something he feels is important, apart from what is reflected in his transcripts, test scores, recommendations, and list of extracurricular activities. This section is important for two reasons: the essay tells the reader how well the student can express his ideas, opinions, and experiences in writing; and, more important, it provides another window into the student's personality.

For more information on the differences between how to approach the short essay and the personal statement, see chapter 6.

Additional Information

Depending on the college, the program the student is applying to, or the student's talents and skills, additional pieces of an application may be required. A public college or university may want proof of residency for that state. An on-campus or alumni interview may be recommended or required. Some colleges might ask for a copy of a graded academic paper from a high school class, while others might ask for a recommendation from a peer or parent. If your child is applying to a program in the arts, or is a talented performing or visual artist, an audition or portfolio may be required or encouraged. A prospective athlete might be asked to submit a résumé of athletic accomplishments and information from a high school coach (note that when it comes to athletics, your high school coach will likely know as early as junior year whether your child is a candidate for recruitment to a college team and will assist with any information requested by a college). Additionally, there may be an honors program or scholarship opportunity that requires an additional essay or the submission of the application by an earlier date. Some schools might require or recommend interviews and suggest sending DVDs, CDs, or slides from students who would like to showcase artistic ability.

Note that larger schools may not offer interviews and may actively discourage students from sending in supplemental information. Each college or university will have its own guidelines and will state them clearly in the application instructions. Just be aware that specific institutional information, or supplements, may exist.

WARNING! DON'T GO OVERBOARD ON THE ADDITIONAL INFO

Although all parents believe that their children are uniquely talented, admissions officers don't have the time or inclination to wade through thick portfolios of artwork, screenplays, the 150-page report Sally submitted for a national science competition, or sports page clippings. If a student would like to showcase a specific talent, he should use restraint. A writer for the school newspaper can choose two or three articles to submit rather than half a dozen. Most important, if a college says not to send any additional materials, then do not send them!

If a student has incredible talent, this will come out in other areas of the application: grades, awards, recommendation letters, and essays. Your child should not waste his time (and that of the admissions officers) by sending a binder with seventy-five photocopies of awards the student has received since she was in first grade—each in an individual holder!

IV. THE COMMON APPLICATION

The Common Application is often the ideal strategy for students. It is a single form used by more than 270 colleges and universities nationwide. (Note, however, that many state schools do not accept it.) The Common Application will enable your child to spend less time filling out multiple forms that ask for the same information. Thus, it leaves more time for reflecting and communicating in applications, crafting essays, and preparing for any interviews that may take place. If three or more schools on your list accept it, then I highly recommend using the Common Application. For a full list of schools that accept the Common Application and to view or download a copy of the application, visit www.commonapp.org.

NEW RULE OF COLLEGE ADMISSIONS: THE COMMON APP IS BEST

Some parents used to think that schools secretly favored students who used their school's application even when they accepted the Common Application. Parents thought this extra effort showed that the student really wanted to go to that school. This was a myth; the schools didn't care which application students submitted.

This is definitely the case today. Each school that accepts the Common App assesses it in the same way as its own application; in fact, some schools have forgone an institutional application altogether and only use the Common Application.

When a school takes both the Common Application and its own, my advice is to use the Common. Why? It takes less work, which means that a student can spend more time refining it. Schools look at either application the same way.

While we often use the Common Application as the model for discussing college applications, you will find that the essentials remain the same, even if your child chooses not to use the Common Application or is applying to schools that accept only their own institutional application.

College-Specific Supplement

If your child is using the Common Application, the college may require a supplement in addition to the application itself. The Common Application instructions include information about which schools require a supplement to complete the application. The supplement may ask the student to restate information already requested in the Common Application, but in a format that the school prefers. Often, it requires an additional essay or responses to short-answer questions. For instance, it may ask the student to articulate why he is applying to that college.

NEW RULE OF COLLEGE ADMISSIONS: IT'S AN ONLINE WORLD AFTER ALL

Most parents recall typing their college applications and essays on a typewriter. I'm sure it won't surprise you to know that this is no longer the norm. The majority of applications today are either submitted online through the college's Web site or via the Common Application Web site at www. commonapp.org. Some students also choose to handwrite on the application form.

If your child is submitting his application via a Web site, be aware that the online application may format differently when printed. An admissions officer will print out your child's application to review it, so check that the hard copy version looks good. Before you click Send, print out the completed online application and proofread carefully.

V. WORKING WITH YOUR HIGH SCHOOL

Every college application is also going to include information that comes from a student's high school, rather than directly from the applicant. Your child may need to arrange to have the following sent from the guidance or college counseling office:

- school report that includes a high school transcript, school profile, and a recommendation from the guidance or college counselor;
- teacher recommendation(s);
- midyear school report (may not be required).

The more organized you are, the easier it will be to make sure you get everything you need from your high school. Make certain that you familiarize yourself with the procedure for requesting this information from your child's school. Try to do this at the end of the junior year so there are no surprises in the fall if you decide to apply for early or rolling admissions, which have early deadlines. Below are some questions you might want to ask your child's guidance office to how they handle and disseminate information to colleges. They may sound nitpicky, but it is very important to know all of the details concerning the process of completing applications and getting them to admissions offices on time. You don't want your child to miss an application deadline because of an administrative snafu.

- How far in advance does a student need to request a transcript in order to meet the application deadlines?
- Does the high school need copies of the school report forms from each application or do they use their own form for all the college applications?
- Is there a fee for sending out transcripts? Does the student need to provide self-addressed envelopes or postage?

- Does the guidance or college office also send out the teacher recommendations or are teachers individually responsible for sending the letters?
- If the high school sends the entire application, is there a deadline for submitting each application to the guidance office that is different from the college deadline? How does the process differ if a student is applying online?
- Does your school have a maximum number of colleges you can apply to? At some schools they limit the number of colleges they will send information to, so you can't apply to more than that.

The important thing to remember is that each high school has an established procedure for handling requests for school reports, recommendations, and transcripts that they have developed over many years. Respect the procedures and deadlines at your child's school.

DON'T PANIC!
WHAT IF I HAVE QUESTIONS ABOUT THE APPLICATION? WILL THE COLLEGE KNOW IF I CALL A FEW TIMES AND PENALIZE MY CHILD?

While some colleges do keep track of phone calls from applicants (or their parents), very few spend time on this. Usually they keep tabs on interested students by tracking the names of kids who attend open houses, campus tours, and programs the colleges host in local areas.

In general, admissions offices prefer to hear questions directly from students, but they understand that schedules may require that a parent calls with an inquiry. Use your judgment and common courtesy and you won't have to worry about getting a reputation as a pest.

VI. TIPS TO SHARE WITH YOUR CHILD

Even if your child already has good work habits, the following tips are helpful to share during the actual writing and editing of college applications. Here are some I like to recommend to parents and students to stay organized and produce a winning application.

- **Divide the work into manageable pieces and set early deadlines.** If your daughter's goal is to get her applications done a month prior to the due date, she will have enough time to accommodate the history paper that took longer than she expected or the illness that lasted for a week.
- **Follow the exact directions on the application.** Whether an admissions officer is reading a dozen applications that day or sixty, she has a certain amount of time she can spend on your child's application. Any time she spends figuring out what your child sent, because it isn't in the format requested, is time taken away from concentrating on your child's accomplishments or reading her essay. You want the people considering the application to focus on the child, so make their job as easy as possible.
- **Proofread.** Remind your child not to rely on her computer's spell-checker. If she is applying online, print out a copy of the application before she submits it, as it will be easier to see any mistakes. Your child should ask a friend, teacher, parent, or anyone else who knows her well, and whose opinion your family respects, to review her application as well.
- **Keep a record of when your child submits each part of the application.** Keep a copy of any application material your child sends in the folders you have created. Most schools will send an acknowledgment that they received an application. Some allow you to check application status through their Web site. If you don't hear from a school that they received your child's application or that it is complete, make sure to follow up with them.

You should contact them early enough to resend anything that might be missing, but remember to give them enough time to organize the huge amount of information they receive near the deadlines. Remember, it is the student's responsibility to make sure each application is complete at each school.

I wish I could promise that by understanding a college application and getting organized, the stress and tension you and your child will experience during the application process would disappear. Despite the best intentions, you and your child will still be nervous about deadlines and requirements. However, getting and staying organized, understanding the guidelines of your child's school, and discussing expectations will keep stress and tension to a minimum.

CHAPTER 5

THE APPLICATION THEME

**Expert Coach: Karen Spencer,
Former Admissions Officer, Georgetown University**

"That girl is going to be president someday!"
"That boy is the next Harrison Ford!"
"She's a world-class cellist *and* a brilliant scientist!"

Whether from bragging parents, neighborhood gossip, or school newspaper articles, we are all familiar with the phrases used to characterize people and give a quick snapshot of their personalities. College admissions officers often rely on the same quick summations when characterizing students they are reviewing. In this chapter you will learn how you and your child can essentially craft this sentence for an admissions committee—by creating a clear "theme" that appears consistently throughout your child's application. It is impossible to sum up seventeen years of a child's life in a college application, so the theme helps focus admissions officers on the key points about your child: what makes him unique and why he would be a great addition to their school.

Understand that there is no literal "theme" to be written on your child's application. You won't find any specific question that asks you to state a theme. Rather, it is a clear, consistent, and compelling description of a student that is demonstrated and reiterated in every part of the application. Our goal in this chapter is for your child's application to have such a strong and consistent theme that a total stranger could read the completed application and immediately write an enthusiastic sentence describing your child. If you can craft such a strong theme, and your child's grades and test scores match those of the schools on his list, then I believe there is a better than 50 percent chance that your child will be admitted. Because the theme needs to be present in every part of the application, I like to say that all roads of the college application process lead to and from the theme. It is no surprise, then, that we address this central topic in the middle chapter of this book!

RULES TO REMEMBER IN THIS CHAPTER

- **Every application needs a theme.** Setting your child apart in the college admissions process requires the articulation of a single theme that transcends the entire application and is visible in every individual part. This enables the admissions committee to view your child in a positive way as "The Kid Who_____."
- **All roads lead to and from the theme.** The application theme should help prepare other pieces of the application, including: determining essay topics, presenting extracurricular activities, deciding whom to ask for letters of recommendation, and practicing for interviews.
- **Be authentic.** Your child's theme should show an admissions committee his real interests, passions, and ambitions and not what he thinks the admissions committee wants to hear. Colleges can see right through inauthentic "hooks," tricks, and obvious brownnosing, and these tactics can hurt rather than help your child.

I. WHY YOUR CHILD'S APPLICATION NEEDS A THEME

To comprehend the importance of an application theme, it is critical to understand how students are assessed by an admissions committee today. The cold, hard truth is that the application your child has spent months creating will be read and assessed by a college admissions office for somewhere between five and thirty minutes. That's it! This is why it is so crucial for your child to stand out, and stand out quickly—particularly if his grades or test scores are average or below average for the schools on his list.

Colleges can vary greatly in their processes for reviewing applications. However, there are some commonalities, including the fact that at most schools, one single admissions officer is assigned to your child's application and will review it first. After that initial review, some schools send every child's folder to a committee meeting for group review, whereas many others send only borderline cases, leaving most decisions to individual admissions officers. This means that your child's application *may* be reviewed by only one person.

If your child is presented to the entire admissions committee, the individual officer who reviewed the application first will do the presenting. Think of the presentation as a Cliffs Notes version of your child's application—an overview of his academics, extracurriculars, and background in a nutshell. This presentation usually takes about five minutes or less. Presenting allows an admissions officer possibly to advocate for a kid he particularly likes, especially if that kid is borderline, or even to vote against a student for some reason or another. Some kids are obvious admits or denies and therefore decided by one admissions officer, and others can be discussed by a committee for thirty minutes or more.

NEW RULE OF COLLEGE ADMISSIONS: THINK BEYOND THE NUMBERS

Often, applicants get passed over by admissions officers because the students *only* meet the grade and SAT requirements of the school. Rejected applicants may have above-average academics and extracurricular activities. It can be different for parents, students, and guidance counselors to understand why this happens. The reason is that students are not admitted to college on numbers alone. As you have seen in earlier chapters, college admissions officers are in the business of creating a school community made up of a variety of students with different backgrounds, interests, talents, and skills. Therefore, the best applications explicitly show where the applicant will likely "fit" into a school's community. The better you craft this message into a theme, the better your child's chances for a positive reception from an admissions committee.

Sometimes it is enough simply to list your child's activities and send a decent essay; however, the more competitive the college admissions process, the more important it is to help the admissions committee understand the student in his totality. In 2002, I had my first selection committee experience at Georgetown. It was early action and I was asked to "present" my first student to the rest of the committee. I began by listing the student's stellar class rank, the number of AP courses he had taken, and his SAT scores, then the chairman stopped me.

"That's nice, Karen," he said, "but we have these statistics in front of us. What we really want to know is what kind of person he is. What has he contributed to his school? Is he going to enliven a classroom? Would he make a good roommate?"

Georgetown already had more applications from exceptional students than it could ever admit. We always said that 85 percent to 90 percent of all applicants were well qualified. They could easily do the work. At the most competitive colleges, the real se-lection criteria are personal qualities, demonstrated academic in-terest, creativity, leadership, and commitment to school and community—on top of an already stellar academic program. With experience, I found that the best source of information about these aspects were the students themselves.

Admissions officers appreciate when students explicitly show where their interests and strengths lie, and, specifically, how these strengths relate to their goals and accomplishments. In other words, they *want* you to demonstrate a clear theme. Admissions officers generally do an excellent job of interpreting applications; however, that doesn't necessarily mean that they have accurately interpreted the living, breathing student author. Students must provide selection committees with the information to know them personally. It is your child's job to make sure that each aspect of the application theme somehow appears in the essays, the extracurric-ular list, the teacher recommendations, the content of the inter-view, and through any other contact with the admissions office.

The applications that made an impression in committee were those that explicitly highlighted why the student was exceptional. A strong application theme also tells the admissions officer the student is very self-aware. Here is how I might have presented "Anita," a student with a clear and compelling interest in science. After reading her essays, activities chart, and letters of recom-mendation, I was able to say the following to my fellow admis-sions officers:

> "Anita has taken her school's most challenging science courses, has done multiple internships at various labs in the city, she's in-terned at a pharmaceutical company and wants to be a research chemist. She works on the literary magazine in addition to the Science Olympiad and wrote a terrific essay about being a sci-ence nerd who also loves poetry. She wants a liberal arts environ-ment so that she can pursue all of her interests and makes a great case for why Georgetown is the place for her to do so."

By demonstrating a clear theme—science—and making her own case for why Georgetown was the right place for her, Anita made herself an easy "yes." Her clear passion and pursuit of that passion in high school implied that she would continue to pursue her interests, participate in activities, and derive meaning from her college experience, too. And that is exactly the kind of person college admissions officers are looking for.

II. ANATOMY OF A THEME

As you saw in the example of Anita, a theme is a clear and consistent "common denominator" running through a student's application both academically and extracurricularly. It is a statement of who a child is and what interests him. It tells what makes him unique. In its preliminary form, the theme should be a paragraph that answers the question, "If the selection committee gave you one minute to tell them anything about yourself before they make their decision, what would you say?" "One minute" is key, as you now know, since committees and admissions officers generally spend a short amount of time with each application. This is the closest a student will come to sitting at the selection committee table itself.

Next, elements of the theme should then be included and reinforced in any or all of the components of the application process. Here is how to accomplish this:

- **Personal Statement.** Include keywords, related experiences, and references to the theme. For instance, a student with a love of animals and a desire to become a teacher may write about an internship with a local veterinarian and how the vet taught her by example.
- **Short-Answer Essays.** Write about academic interests, extracurriculars, volunteer activities, jobs, or other experiences related to the theme.
- **Activities Chart.** Prioritize activities related to the theme at the top of the chart to show their significance. A girl with a theme of

politics may list student government, debate team, and a summer job on Capitol Hill as her top three activities before mentioning that she is also on the volleyball team. A boy with a theme of finance may prioritize his membership in Future Business Leaders of America, volunteer activities with Junior Achievement, and a position as business reporter for the school newspaper. Next he might list his other activities, such as working in a soup kitchen and playing viola.

- **Letters of Recommendation.** While you can't write recommendation letters yourself, you can select teachers related to the subjects or extracurricular interests that relate to your child's theme. This will show that your child has forged relationships with adults who are passionate about the same interests. For instance, a boy with a theme of technology who wants to major in computer science may request a recommendation from the teacher who leads the computer club. A girl who loves literature and edits the yearbook may request a letter of recommendation from her English teacher.
- **Interviews.** Your child can incorporate the application theme into college interviews by being prepared to tell anecdotes related to the theme. For instance, if an interviewer asks a student why she wants to attend the University of Southern California and her theme involves urban planning, she may talk about her love for cities and her desire to become active in USC's volunteer work in poverty-stricken neighborhoods in Los Angeles.

The best way to understand how to craft and include a strong theme in the college application process is to look at some examples. Themes, as you will see, are as varied as the students themselves. Remember, these exact words may not appear in the application directly, but variations may emerge in personal statements, short-answer essays, and interview comments.

Here is an example of an excellent theme.

"I am an English fanatic who is fascinated by the works of Shakespeare. My interests have led me to pursue study in England and

> **initiate our first ever Shakespeare Day at my high school, and I hope to continue my studies in Shakespeare with the same level of enthusiasm in college."**

This theme is strong because it paints a clear picture of the student's passion and it has energy. It also gives the admissions officer a clear idea of how this student will contribute to a campus community. For instance, she is the one who might bring new life to the flailing Shakespeare Society or ignite an English classroom. In an application, this theme could be reflected in the following ways:

- Shakespeare Day listed as a leadership role on the activities chart;
- excellent grades in English;
- strong test scores on the SAT I writing section;
- recommendation from an English or theater teacher discussing this student's passion;
- discussing her favorite Shakespeare plays during a college interview.

Now let's look at a weak example of a theme.

> **"I am a hardworking student. My family relies on me to be a good role model to my brothers and cousins. I am a good friend, and my teachers like me for my participation in class. On the hockey team, I am respected for being a loyal teammate. I would like to be a psychology major in college because I like understanding what makes people tick."**

This is not a strong theme because it is nebulous: there are no specific, clear examples of what this child is passionate about or what he might want to do in college. He may or may not want to pursue hockey. He may or may not be a psychology major because he doesn't show any true passion for it. With the same elements, this student could have conceived a better theme to incorporate into his application, such as:

"I am a team player. From my large extended family to my hockey team to my academic classes, I am committed to group work and dynamics. I believe that community is extremely important, and I always look for ways to contribute to the various committees of which I am a part. For this reason, I am interested in pursuing a psychology major, to study group dynamics and one day research ways for people to build stronger communities."

With a strong theme of community and teamwork, this student could incorporate his theme in the following ways:

- show a variety of team sports and community volunteer events on his activities chart;
- write a personal statement that discusses the value of community or teamwork;
- include a letter of recommendation from a hockey coach that praises this student for his sportsmanship and enthusiasm for the team.

I genuinely believe that almost all students can craft a meaningful theme by "connecting the dots" among activities, interests, and future goals. Some themes will certainly be stronger than others, but finding a theme is possible with some thought and creativity.

NEW RULE OF COLLEGE ADMISSIONS: BE REAL!

Contrary to popular belief, admissions officers love students who share their true personalities in an application. Kids shouldn't reveal themselves to be generic; encourage your child to be real and different—quirks and all! The application theme, and the application developed as a result, should be a reflection of the student's authentic self. Don't nudge your child to try to tell the colleges what you think they want to hear. Instead, prompt your child to tell colleges what he wants the schools to know. As you have seen in the examples of good themes, college admissions officers like to see genuine passion, interest, and self-awareness. I promise you this will make a more lasting impression.

For example, the best essay I ever read was a funny one about the small town in Indiana where the student grew up and how it contributed to his personality and interests. One of the best lines was, "My town's idea of affirmative action is hiring someone without a farmer's tan." The student never once had to say, 'I am" or "I believe" because he showed me who he was by what he chose to write about (his background) and his honesty. His end point was to make the most of where you are because greatness can be found in the most unusual places. I remembered him as "the awesome kid from small-town Indiana who wrote about what it was like to live in a small town."

PARENT TO-DO: HELPING YOUR CHILD DETERMINE AN APPLICATION THEME

Here are three steps to help you craft a theme with your child:

1. Work with your child to fill in the blanks in this formula:
Strongest academic subject: _____
+
Specific example of academic success: _____
_____
+
Demonstrated extracurricular interest (ideally in a related area):
_____
_____
+
Idea of future plans (college major or future career—ideally somehow related to the above): _____
_____

Now, look for "common denominators" that connect the above answers. The common denominators are words, phrases, concepts, or ideas that link the above answers into a distinguishable, easy-to-notice application theme. Here is a list of some "common denominators." Circle any that may help serve as a thread among the factors you and your child listed above:

Activism	Engineering	Performance
Adventure	Entrepreneurship	People
Agriculture	Environmental issues	Politics
Animals	Ethnicity	Religion
Architecture	Experimentation	Science
Art	Finance	Social justice
Business	Journalism	Sports
Children	Languages	Teaching
Communication	Law	Technology
Community	Leadership	Travel
Coordination	Medicine	Urban issues
Creativity	Music	Women's issues
Design	Organization	World issues

By identifying key words, like the ones above, your child can incorporate these into his short-answer essays, personal statements, interview answers, and other elements of the application process to make sure he can be described clearly and positively by an admissions officer.

2. Another angle is to ask the questions below and look for key words in your child's answers. As in the first exercise, the goal is to connect the dots among your child's interests and achievements and link them into a consistent theme. Essentially, you are looking for patterns. You can also refer back to the self-assessment exercises in chapter 1 and look for common denominators and key words in your child's answers there.

Ask your child to complete these sentences. Do not be concerned if he doesn't have compelling answers to all of the sentences, but focus on the areas where your child clearly "lights up" and becomes excited. Those are the most likely places to find a compelling theme.

- I am enthusiastic about _____.
- My friends say that the most unique or best thing about me is

  _____.
- A unique accomplishment of mine involves _____.
- I'm proud of the time that I _____.
- I really care about _____.
- A common denominator/similar aspect to my academics and activities is _____.
- In college, I would really like to _____.
- I chose the particular activities I've participated in because

  _____.
- In the future I hope to _____.

3. The final step is for your child to come up with a one-minute description of what makes him unique and how he will contribute his uniqueness to the particular schools he wants to attend. Once you have identified some patterns and themes, have your child write a short paragraph or several bullet points that highlight the qualities, situations, or accomplishments he wants to showcase in his applications. Remind your student that the goal is not to say every little thing, or to emphasize less meaningful activities or accomplishments. The more focused the theme, the more effective it will be.

My child's theme is:

_____

_____

_____

_____

DON'T PANIC! WHAT IF MY CHILD JUST DOESN'T SEEM TO HAVE A THEME?

It is true that for some kids a theme is easy to determine and for some it's more difficult. If your student is like the majority of students whose theme is not as cohesive as you might wish, don't panic. Students often struggle with identifying the aspects that make them unique. Remind your child that while other students might also enjoy directing theater, or have intense school spirit, or participate often in class, not everyone will embody all of these qualities simultaneously. Although others may share similar interests, *no one* else will have the personal insight and experience that your child has.

Colleges want to fill their classes with unique individuals who demonstrate curiosity and a thirst for higher education. So, if your child is struggling with finding one theme, the next best thing is to show clear and consistent interest and achievement in a few areas. You can help your child to draw out a few key threads that run through the entire application. This means that if your child has tried a variety of different activities and is uncertain about his future plans, then at least make sure your child is clear about his top interest in academics and his top interest extracurricularly and tie these to why he wants to attend a certain college. Then, show how your child has some passion for his interests and a desire to explore more pursuits in college. For instance, "This is a kid whose favorite subject is anything related to science and she loves to play soccer. She would like to attend a college where she can pursue both interests and explore others."

At the very least, be sure that your child's application consistently promotes the fact that he wants to attend college to be an active participant and contributor, and not just attend a few random classes and walk away with a degree.

Just *Don't* Do It: "Tricks and Hooks"

There is one huge caveat in all of my advice about crafting a theme: resist the temptation to create an application theme that is invented for the sake of "outsmarting" the colleges. While potentially demoralizing to the student, an inaccurate, irrelevant, or fabricated theme will also detract from your student's accomplishments. I once worked with a family who, after looking at their daughter's profile, said, "She wants to be a biology major and eventually become a doctor, but we know that lots of kids want to study biology and go premed. Should she apply as a sociology major instead?" The student's curriculum and activities revealed a strong lineup of biology courses, a continuous string of lab internships in medicine and biology, and extracurricular activities in science. It listed only one measly semester-long sociology course. I explained that their daughter's best shot at a top college was in the subject where she's already demonstrated so much interest and passion. Majoring in sociology didn't make sense to the student, nor would it to the admissions officers who would read the application.

In another instance, I once met the mother of a high school senior who quietly announced, "We've finally found her hook." "Hooks," in college admissions parlance, refer to special qualities that are particularly appealing to college admissions offices. Hooks might include: outstanding athletic or musical accomplishments, kinship with the chairman of the board of trustees, or a national award. The mother explained that her forefathers had fled Eastern Europe during World War Two with a religious artifact, in hopes of keeping it safe. The previous summer, they determined it was time to return the artifact to its homeland. The family brought it back to great festivity and fanfare, of which the daughter was part.

"And how does this help us to know your daughter better?" I asked.

There was no reply. If her daughter had researched the artifact, initiated contact with the religious community abroad, if her visit enabled her to study religion, or perhaps if she had performed community service that coincided with her academic or personal areas of interest, then the experience may have been a perfectly legitimate component of her application theme. Merely pulling a meaningful experience out of a student's life and shaping a theme around it will not benefit the student. In fact, it will hurt the student because it makes him look inauthentic.

Case Study

Let's walk through the full process of a theme through a case study from my experience as an admissions officer. As I have mentioned, I was always grateful to students who made it easy for me to understand their special talents and strengths through repetition and elaboration. Unfortunately, it was more often I had to present a student during selection committee using a string of unrelated accomplishments. This was the case with "Jonathan." Jonathan is on the staff of the literary magazine and captain of the rugby team. His chemistry teacher says Jonathan's one of the best he's ever seen, and Jonathan is in the top 10 percent of the class. He wrote his essay about his trip to the Dominican Republic, and he says he wants to major in English. To help illustrate this example, here is a summary of Jonathan's accomplishments.

Partial list of Jonathan's application information:

- public high school;
- top 10 percent of class;
- enrolled in three AP courses (calculus, English, Spanish);
- captain of rugby team;
- chess team member;
- community service club committee head;
- literary magazine staff;
- essay about visiting the Dominican Republic—a travelogue;
- "Why Georgetown?" essay is vague, briefly mentions English department.

When it was time to present Jonathan's file to the selection committee, I had a tough time. Here's a guy who wants to become an English major, and while he has some nice experience in the subject (AP English, literary magazine staff), he hasn't bothered to explain how his experiences led to a pursuit of English. His best opportunity to do so was in his essay. However, he chose instead to tell us about his visit to the sunny beaches of the Dominican Republic. If Jonathan had been more aware of the importance of the application theme, he might have positioned himself differently. This might have been Jonathan's overall application theme:

> **"As a result of my classroom experiences and my work as the poetry editor for the literary magazine, I have a strong interest in pursuing English as a major, focusing on American writers. I also have an interest in Latin American culture, which I have pursued in my AP Spanish class and family trips to the region. I hope to minor in Spanish."**

Using this as a basis, Jonathan could have ensured his theme was explicitly revealed within the various components of the application. For instance, he might have written about his interest in Latin American studies in his personal statement and focused on reasons behind majoring in English in his "Why Georgetown?" essay. In his extracurricular list, he might have prioritized those activities that related to his theme, such as the literary magazine or perhaps community service club that involved teaching reading skills. He might have specifically sought recommendations from his English and Spanish teachers, and reiterated the theme during his interview when talking about academic and personal interests.

As you can see, the job of the theme is to pull everything together into a compelling "pitch" for your child. Merely telling the facts and hoping an admissions officer will "get it" just isn't enough. You have to show that your child has interests and goals and that he will be a contributing member of a college community. There are a million and one ways to do this—as unique as the applicants themselves—but a theme must be communicated in order to make your child's application stand out. Five minutes at an admissions committee meeting could determine your child's future. By creating a theme, your child is doing the best he can to help those five minutes result in an acceptance.

Many aspects of the college application contribute to its overall success. But, as you have seen in this chapter, *how* you present information can be just as important as the information itself. The theme is a great beginning, and in the following chapters, you will have the opportunity to apply your child's theme and build an exceptionally presented application, one step at a time.

CHAPTER 6

ESSAYS AND PERSONAL STATEMENTS

Expert Coach: Scott Ham,
Former Admissions Officer, Northwestern University

Contrary to what you might think, colleges do not want an entire school of A students with 1600s on their SATs. How boring! As you have learned, college admissions committees are faced with the task of creating diverse communities, including students of various ethnicities, geographic backgrounds, athletic talents, political thoughts, favorite movies, religious beliefs, senses of humor, artistic abilities, and more. To do this, they have to learn as much as they can about the students applying to their school.

Of course they have grades, course schedules, lists of activities/awards/honors, recommendation letters, and maybe even notes from an interview—and this information is important in determining fit between the school and the student and a student's chances for success on any given campus. However, none of this says much about a student's *personality*. Nor does it help to distinguish the applicant from others. The college essay is the only time the admissions committee gets to hear directly from the student, in his own voice.

While many students dread writing the essay, I think students should approach it enthusiastically because of the amazing opportunity it provides. The essay is a chance for students to share what is meaningful, important, humorous, unique, or challenging in their lives. It gives applicants an opportunity to make a connection between the other aspects of the application—why they participated in a specific activity, why they want to study a specific subject, why they are applying to a specific institution. The essay is the one place in the application where students get to be themselves, represent how they think, and explain what they want to do during their college career. It is also the only place on the application where the student gets to speak directly to the admissions committee and make his case.

RULES TO REMEMBER IN THIS CHAPTER

- **The keyword in personal statement is *personal*.** Essays and short-answer questions are the best opportunity for your child to articulate his unique application theme, thus showing his personality and distinguishing himself from the rest of the pool. Since there are few opportunities to personalize the application, it is critical to maximize the limited words allowed for in the college essay.
- **Start as early as possible and proceed step-by-step.** To make the essay writing process as smooth as possible, help your child to brainstorm, outline, write, and revise—and not leave out any of these crucial steps.
- **Answer the "why."** In a college essay, the analysis carries far more weight than the description. Remind your child to "show, not tell" and reveal his opinions, goals, dreams, and motivations rather than "reporting" his life story.
- **Know what pitfalls to avoid.** Many students attempt to write what they believe college admissions officers want to hear. This is an unfortunate trap for many. It is more important for the student to be real. He should use natural language and provide real insight, while never bragging, making excuses, or tackling too much material.

I. GETTING STARTED

In my opinion, one of the most important things you can do is to help your child adopt a positive attitude about the essay. It is not a torture sentence! You can frame the essay as the one chance your child has to shine, to stand out, to win over those admissions people. It's a chance to express himself, to help the college get to know him better, and to show a small piece of what makes him unique. Writing is certainly hard work, but the result of this particular hard work can be acceptance to a great school.

The best way to reduce essay writing stress, of course, is to start early. Because kids dread the essay writing process, they put it off to the last minute. This forces students to rush the process, not leaving enough time for the multiple steps: picking a question and topic, brainstorming ideas and examples, writing a rough draft, and revising the essay multiple times. If you take nothing else away from this chapter, remember to encourage your child to start the essay writing process as early as possible. Students may even want to start thinking about college essays in the summer between the junior and senior years.

Also be aware that your child may be shy about sharing the essay with you. Students sometimes think that parents will think their real feelings are not important, or they may be embarrassed to reveal their opinions or dreams. Remember to respect your child through this often stressful and emotional process.

DON'T PANIC! LATE STARTERS

If you are reading this chapter and your child's essay is due in the next few weeks, do your best to follow the steps below in an accelerated manner. One good option is to dedicate a certain number of hours each day to essay brainstorming, writing, and editing, so your child doesn't cram everything into one weekend and become burnt out. Take a deep breath and follow the steps to make sure even a quickly written essay is still structurally sound, has a good topic, addresses the essay question, and is free of mistakes.

II. UNDERSTANDING THE ASSIGNMENTS

Before we discuss the writing process, let's take a close look at the kind of writing samples colleges want to see. As with many aspects of the application process, schools vary widely in their requirements. Some colleges and universities will ask for several different types of writing samples, giving students an opportunity to show their abilities and talents based on the different types of questions and how they respond to each. Some schools require only one essay. Others may ask for a graded paper from a class assignment. It is important to look into the requirements for each college application before a single word hits the page. Your child needs to know what is expected for each school on his list, and he needs to leave enough time to complete each writing component of every application.

NEW RULE OF COLLEGE ADMISSIONS: DON'T FORGET THE THEME

As you learned in the previous chapter, college essays also serve as important opportunities to express and support a student's overall theme—the overarching thread that runs through the application. If the essays do not support the theme, it is more difficult for an admissions committee to fully understand why the student is unique and a good fit for its school. The theme can be successfully incorporated no matter what the essay requirements of each school.

Remind your child to think about incorporating his theme into every step of the essay writing process. You will find many pointers on this in the sections below.

The College Essay

The most common form of written response is the college essay or personal statement. For simplicity, this will be referred to as "the essay." This is what every student seems to dread the most— typically a 250 to 500 word statement requiring personal reflection and analysis.

What are college admissions officers looking for when they read essays? Quite simply, they want to get to know a student's personality. As I think back to admissions decisions we made at Northwestern, often they were determined by how well we got to know a student through her essay. Think about it from the admissions officer's perspective: when you are reading thousands of applications, you appreciate most the students who share more of themselves and tell a compelling story or share an honest emotion. It's like a personal letter from a friend as opposed to a form letter.

Types of Questions

Colleges will typically ask two types of questions: open-ended questions and analytical questions. Depending on the question your student chooses to answer, the options for a topic may be very broad or exceptionally specific.

Open-ended questions such as, "Tell us about a meaningful experience, and why it is meaningful to you," give students latitude in their response. They get to define what is meaningful, determine what event is meaningful to them in that context, and then analyze why it was meaningful given the context of their definition. Students often struggle with such open-ended questions because they try to include too much information and too much description, leaving no room for analysis. When approaching an open-ended question, students should take the time to pick one isolated event, experience, or occurrence and explore that one unique point. Students need to be reminded that the essay is not their life story in five hundred words or less. Remind your child that the best way for the admissions committee to get to know him on a more personal level is to give personal insight on the topic, not description.

For the analytical questions, students will typically be given a quote, portion of an essay, mission statement, or poem and asked to take a stance and explain how their beliefs fit with their stance. Students struggle with these types of questions because they treat them like a term paper for school, rather than an exploration of their beliefs.

Analytical questions are meant to encourage students to take the time to consider what they really think and feel on a given issue. By providing personal insight into their thoughts and beliefs, students permit the admissions committee to learn about their attitudes, work and study habits, and goals for the future. The best way for students to explain their stance is by using real examples from their own lives and experiences. Again, it is important to remind students that answering the "Why?" portion of the response is crucial. Without the analysis of why they took the position, the essay becomes a compilation of facts with no personal foundation for the admissions committee to learn more about them.

The Essay Format

When writing the essay, it is easiest to look at it in three parts: the introduction, the body, and the conclusion. Because college essays typically have a word limit, students need to be direct and concise. The essay differs from traditional high school papers in that it doesn't have to be the standard five-paragraph essays. In a college essay:

- **The introduction** needs to be compelling and set up the thesis statement. What is the main message the student is trying to convey?
- **The body** needs to define and support the thesis statement. The body of the essay is the personal reflection and analysis that supports the thesis statement. The body should not read like a list of awards, activities, or honors, but rather as an investigation into the key concept that the student is trying to convey. Unlike high school essays that require three paragraphs in the body, there is no formula for the body of a college essay.

- **The conclusion** needs to go beyond a summary and provide a final insight.

Each of these sections will be discussed in detail in the "Writing Process" section below.

Short-Answer Essays

Many colleges and universities have short-answer statements as part of their application, in addition to the personal statement described above. These questions prompt students to respond to less in-depth questions, in just a few sentences—usually one hundred words or fewer. While both types of essays are personal, short-answer essays do not require the same reflection and analysis as the longer personal statements. Short-answer essays are meant to give the admissions committee a snapshot of the student's personality, as well as the student's ability to form a response in a concise and direct manner.

Short essay questions might include:

- "Please describe which of your activities (extracurricular and personal activities or work experience) has been most meaningful and why."
- "What did you do last Sunday, or the Sunday before that, or the Sunday before that?"

WARNING! OBEY THE WORD LIMIT

The biggest mistake students make on the short-essay statements is trying to say too much. Most schools that ask for short-answer statements will ask for students to respond in the space provided. If students are using a paper application, they often write so small, you need a magnifying glass to read it. Or they tape a tiny-printed response in the space provided. Some colleges ask for double-spaced, 12-point "standard" font, which generally includes Times New Roman, Courier, or Arial, but many applications do not specify. If nothing is specified, your child should still go with the 12-

point standard font. When reading hundreds of applications daily, nothing is more irritating to a member of the admissions committee than straining to read tiny print.

While the online application formats the correct font and type size, those students who complete the online application often don't realize their response was truncated after one hundred words. They end up submitting an incomplete response. On the short-essay questions, remind your child the emphasis is on the word *short*.

P.S.: This is good advice for the longer personal statement as well. Remind your child to stick to the word count or the end of his essay may never be seen.

Other Writing Submissions

Some institutions ask students to explain why they are applying to that specific institution. This is a variation on the short-answer essay. The "Why are you applying?" question is a chance for students to show that they have done their research and can provide specific reasoning for wanting to attend that school. It is important that students spend some time thinking creatively about this question before responding. (Hint: If your child is struggling with a reason to attend a specific school, it might not be the best fit.)

Responses to these types of questions should be as specific, and as personal, as possible. This is the applicant's direct opportunity to explain why he and the school are a perfect match, so it's important to give a specific and persuasive answer. Let's look at some dos and don'ts.

If your daughter is attracted to a specific school because of its location, faculty, and student body:

Don't simply answer the question with "location, faculty, and student body." This is generic and does not distinguish your daughter's interest. And it could be said about any school in the country.

Do encourage your daughter to be specific. What exactly is it about the school's location, faculty, and student body that appeal to her? This is a terrific opportunity to reiterate her theme. For instance, if your daughter is politically active and wants to attend American University in Washington, DC, she can write about her attraction to attending school in the nation's capital and attending guest lectures from politicians and visiting dignitaries. If she is interested in animals and wants to be a veterinarian, she may tie this to her desire to attend a college in a rural location and interact with other students who are interested in nature and wildlife.

Do make sure your child shows that she has done her homework about the school and is excited about possibly attending. It's important for her to show that she has taken the time and effort to learn more about the school than simply reading a brochure and surfing the college's Web site. She can mention specific departments, clubs, community events, or other factors that relate to her unique talents and interests. For instance, she might mention a desire to sing in a particular a cappella group or mention an intended major that is particularly popular at that school.

WARNING! SPELLING COUNTS

Make sure that your student has the correct name and spelling of the institution. (There is no such thing as the University of Indiana, it is Indiana University; and it is Notre Dame, not Noter Dame.) It's also important you know where exactly the institution is located and the surrounding area. When I was on the admissions committee at Northwestern University in Evanston, Illinois, I read several "Why are you applying to Northwestern?" statements talking about our location in *Evansville* or our great proximity to *Lake Erie* (Evanston and Chicago are both on the shore of Lake Michigan). And most important, if your student is applying to more than one school that asks this question, make sure he writes a completely different response for each school. Nothing will hurt a student's chances for admission more than saying it has been a lifelong dream to go to Cornell when she is applying to Duke!

Artist's Statements

If you have a student who is interested in applying to a fine arts program, it is likely that he will be asked to submit an "artist's statement" in addition to the essay and short-answer questions. This statement is meant to show the admissions committee what inspires that student's work. It often will allow the student to explain slides in the portfolio, media used in the work's creation, or reasoning for choosing a piece to explore. A student may be asked to explain his interest in art or in the specific type of art he plans to pursue (e.g., sculpture, portraiture, textile design). Sometimes the artist's statement takes the form of a written guide to what the portfolio review committee will be considering. Since the artist's statement is so specific to the portfolio, note that it cannot be used as a substitute for the college essay.

WARNING! DON'T REUSE HIGH SCHOOL PAPERS

While it was previously mentioned that some colleges and universities request a high school paper, most institutions will want to see original writing samples, tied to specific essay questions, on their applications. Too often students believe that a well-written high school English paper will suffice for a college application essay. This is rarely the case.

Unless the high school class assignment is to respond to a college essay question, do not use a previously written high school paper for an application. The questions posed by the different colleges and universities are meant to have students explore specific aspects of their lives in preparation for college. The recycled paper will likely miss certain aspects of the question and ultimately will not answer the question. The application will be weaker in comparison to other applicants who have taken time to write specifically to the essay prompt. Sorry, there are no shortcuts!

III. THE ESSAY WRITING PROCESS

Now that you have an understanding of what colleges are looking for in applicant essays and what types of essays are required, let's look at a step-by-step process for guiding your child through the process of writing the most challenging submission—the personal statement essay. You will find many tips, ideas, and examples. I urge you to work closely with your child to find the strategies that make the process the least stressful and most productive. I know that this can be tough and tense, so remind your child to keep his eyes on the prize: at the end of this process he may be accepted to the college of his dreams.

Step 1: Brainstorm essay topics

Many students believe that getting started is simply carving out a few hours over the weekend to sit down and write an essay that will wow an admissions committee. Yet the process really needs to begin long before the writing starts—with brainstorming.

Brainstorming helps students come up with a wide variety of ideas, concepts, words, phrases, feelings, and examples that may be used in the final essay. Ultimately, the goal of brainstorming is for your child to find the "slice of life" that best showcases what makes him stand out. Each student has something that makes his or her application different; use the essay to help bring that individuality to light.

To give you an idea of what I mean, here are two examples that really stood out. These are creative examples of "slices of life" that allowed the student to show individuality and find a jumping-off point for an exploration of his or her personality.

- A young lady wrote about her hair: "I've done everything I can to it. I have dyed it, cut it, grown it, and ironed it, but it is still there. I am talking about my bright red frizzy wiry hair." She then proceeded to tell about how each element of her hair tied to a different personality trait or key thought.

- A young man was born in China and moved to Texas when he was three months old. In writing about his Chinese-American "dual life" he told a story about grilling steak in his family's yard and then going inside the house to eat it with chopsticks.

To help your child find his own compelling topic, incident, or trait, you can try several brainstorming techniques. Some students will want to try all of these techniques; others will settle on one that works for them. The important thing for students to remember is that essay writing is a *process* with several steps.

Brainstorming can begin as soon as your child first has the application. Coming up with the specifics of what to include in the final essay may take weeks or even months, so planning ahead and starting early are important. Also remind your child to keep his application theme in mind while brainstorming. What follows are some of the most common and effective brainstorming strategies.

Mind Dump

This strategy is a great place to begin. The mind dump is exactly what the name suggests—getting everything that comes to mind "dumped" out on paper. It is meant not only to flush out ideas for the essay, but also to purge the student's mind of anything that might be preventing a clear focus. It is not necessarily a focused approach, but it is helpful for a student who is feeling anxious, frustrated, or blank. Mind dumping gets ideas flowing; there are no "wrong" ways to mind dump. Here is an exercise to help.

To-Do: Mind Dump Exercise

1. **Set the Mood.** To get the mind dump started, the student should be relaxed and in a good mood. He may want to do a mind dump after listening to a favorite song, watching a TV show, or playing a video game.
2. **Get Quiet.** Once the student feels relaxed, he should ta¹ several pieces of paper and sit in a quiet space for ⁻¹ five minutes (or longer, if desired). Pick a ᵗ quiet spot without distractions.

3. **Let the Dump Begin.** During this time, encourage your child to write down whatever comes to mind—themes for the essay, experiences that are meaningful, reasons he chose the topic, fears about writing this essay, concern about the future, goals, dreams, friends, dates—*anything* that comes to mind.

4. **Categorize.** Next the student should organize the "dumped" words and phrases into category columns. This is where you can help. Categories might include: dreams, experiences, goals, activities, people, future plans, and so on. When possible, be sure to include a category that relates to your child's application theme. For example, a category such as "communication," "leadership," "creativity," or "scientific exploration" might be a good. Adding such a category will help your child be sure to incorporate the theme into his essay. Once the categories are completed, your child will likely have some concrete points and examples to give the essay direction. If your student does not have enough points to start building an outline, he should try another mind dump or another of the brainstorming techniques.

Journaling

This form of brainstorming is one of the most useful techniques, not only for generating ideas for the essay, but also for preparing to write in general. Many teenagers already keep a personal journal of life events, goals, and dreams, so it's a comfortable format as well. For those students who have kept a journal, the essay writing process is often less stressful. They have records of their thoughts and feelings after different events. They have already spent time analyzing what happened and can draw from that analysis to determine the best course for the college essay. If your daughter has been keeping a journal, you may want to encourage her to look through past entries to see if there is something in the journal that would be appropriate to share with the admissions committee.

Students who have not kept a regular journal, or those who do not feel comfortable sharing past entries with an admissions committee (or with a parent), may want to consider starting a journal of daily events and their reactions to those events. You can encourage this practice as early as you'd like, but I find this a particularly helpful strategy for students to undertake during junior year or the summer before senior year to get used to the journaling habit. The entries do not need to be long, nor do they need to be philosophically significant. The purpose of journaling is to get students to feel comfortable writing about themselves, their feelings, and the analysis of those feelings. The more comfortable students are with writing about themselves, the easier the college essay will be.

Note Cards

This strategy is a blend between the mind dump and journaling, and requires students to carry around a stack of note cards. As different ideas, phrases, concepts, events, and conversations occur, students would write whatever comes to mind on a note card. Each note card would hold one idea/phrase/event/concept. After several days (or weeks) of keeping these note cards, students would then be able to organize them into a working outline for the essay. The beauty of note cards is the flexibility it allows students in creating a fluid thought process. If after the note cards are organized, something seems out of place, it is very easy to move the note card to a more appropriate position. Note cards can also be kept almost anywhere, so anytime an idea strikes, the student can jot it down.

Discussion

Perhaps the most common form of brainstorming is discussion. All students are stressed about writing college essays, and it will be a common topic for discussion throughout the application process. Students should be encouraged to take advantage of this dialogue with family and friends. Discussing different topics and perspectives can help flesh out a student's true feelings on an issue. It can also help to avoid duplication of topics. The important thing to remember about discussions is to take some sort of notes during them. Many times great ideas are generated during conversations with friends and family, but once the conversation ends, the ideas are lost. Whether your student uses note cards or a journal entry, it is important that these intellectual strides are not lost after the conversation's conclusion.

Concluding the Brainstorming Process

Whatever brainstorming process or processes your child has chosen, the final step is to look for themes. As you did in the "Categorize" step of the mind dump, work with your child to organize his brainstorming into one or several themes that he wants to relate in the essay. If many themes come up, your child can brainstorm again on each theme to see which he feels is most representative of his personality or which he has the strongest thoughts or feelings about.

Step 2. Choose the best topic and create an outline

Selecting a topic is often easier said than done. Students need first to select the essay question or "prompt" that most closely aligns with the message they want to convey. Most colleges and universities will give students a choice of questions to select from. As mentioned, the main gist of most of the topics is to describe something (a person, event, place, or other topic) that is meaningful to the student and to explain why. Ultimately, your child needs to decide which question will allow him to share his most unique attributes with the admission committee.

DON'T PANIC! CAN MY CHILD CHOOSE THE "WRONG" ESSAY QUESTION?

Because students are given a choice of questions, they often falsely assume the admissions committee wants them to answer one specific question, and if they pick the wrong one, they will be penalized. This is truly not the case. If an institution were looking for every student to answer the same question so they could judge applicants on a level playing field, they would ask only one question. Admissions committees will often offer more than one essay option to students so that their reading load has some variation in topic and scope. Reading thousands of essays with the same essay prompt can become monotonous, so if your student has a choice of topics, he should feel free to choose the one that most closely aligns with his own personal experiences. There is no "wrong" question to choose.

WARNING! THE CHOICE (AND THE ESSAY) IS YOUR CHILD'S—NOT YOURS

Because the best essays are those that analyze a personal experience and why that experience was significant, it is important that your child answer the essay question of *his* choice—and not yours. As a parent, you may see things you think are unique and worthy of being the subject of a college essay. However, it is likely that your child does not see things the same way. Most students struggle to see themselves in the same light as their parents do.

If you try to persuade your daughter to write a certain essay, she may attempt to please you, but it will not be the essay that best suits her personality and skills. As you work with your child to select an essay question, keep an open line of communication. If your child resists your help, don't be discouraged. Let your student know you are there for support and encouragement, but understand that kids may need to do some soul searching before being able to fully discuss their choices.

Answering the "Why"

Once the question is chosen, your child needs to come up with a specific response. The hardest part about choosing a specific topic for the essay response is finding a way to highlight a student's strengths without repeating information already included in the application materials and without selecting a trite topic. The key to a good essay topic is picking a question that allows the student to provide some description, in combination with strong analysis of that description. Thorough description is critical for a successful essay, but the reasons, emotions, and examples that answer the "why" will create the body of your student's essay.

Here are is an example of a single topic choice and good and bad "why" answers to the question, "Describe an event that was meaningful to you and explain why it was meaningful."

Topic selection: Volunteering at a summer camp for kids with cancer. *This is a good topic choice because it allows for examples of children the student met, experiences he had, and emotions he felt.*

Bad "Why": This was meaningful because all kids should be able to have fun and play even if they are terminally ill. *This is a bad "why" because it is relatively trite and does not show how this experience was important to you in particular.*

Better "Why": This was meaningful because my grandfather recently died of cancer and I always thought of the disease as something that affected elderly people. Since my future plans involve a desire to work on public policy issues, I will now be more aware of the multiple populations that can be affected by a single issue. *This is a better "why" because it brings in a personal experience and also shows the student's future career interest.*

Outlining

Once the brainstorming is complete and the chosen topic has specific examples for support, students should create a detailed outline. The outline should clearly move the student from introduction to conclusion, with a strong thesis statement and examples that provide personal insight and analysis. A guide to creating each section of the outline appears below.

Step 3. Create a compelling opener

The introduction serves as a first impression of the student's personality for the admissions committee. It is crucial that the opening sentence grab the attention of committee members. Students should look at ways to introduce their topic so that the reader wants to find out more. If your student is responding to the prompt: "Tell us about a meaningful experience and why it is meaningful," he should not begin the essay by saying, "My most meaningful experience was the mission trip to Mexico I took in eighth grade." Boring! This statement does nothing to draw the reader into the essay, nor does it help distinguish the student from the thousands of other applicants who have had similar experiences. The purpose of the introductory paragraph is to get the reader interested in what the student has to say. If there is nothing to draw the reader into the essay, the admissions committee members will spend less time getting to know the student through the essay.

Options for more dynamic opening sentences for the same essay might be:

- "I'd never been away from home for more than an overnight sleepover at my neighbor's house."
- "*Hola!* and *Gracias!* were the extent of my Spanish as I boarded the plane to Mexico."
- "I don't know if I've ever been as excited and as nervous at the same time."

These opening sentences draw the reader into the story. The reader wants to find out what is going to happen and how it affected the student. Still, students should be cautioned not to take the opening sentence or the introductory paragraph too far. Making outlandish claims or using gimmicks can have the same impact as a dry, routine opening—the admissions committee spends less time getting to know the student.

The introductory paragraph also gives direction and structure to the essay. A student should use the introduction to set up any history that will be pertinent to his thesis, and the thesis should flow from that information. While the body of the essay will be analytical, the introduction should contain enough description to give meaning to the analysis that follows. It may help students to think of the introduction as the "What" in their essays. What are they going to talk about in the essay? What prompted an interest in this event? What do they hope to get out of the experience? By establishing the "What" in the introduction, they can use the body of the essay to discuss the all-important "Why."

Thesis Statement

Students often struggle with determining their essay's thesis statement, or focal point. Because so many teenagers resist talking about themselves, the thesis is often muddied by too much description. The outline should organize the paper in such a way that the description and background information are included in the introductory paragraph. The introduction should take the reader to a specific thesis, or focus, that will be supported by examples in the body of the essay. The thesis statement is most commonly found at the end of the introductory paragraph.

So, how does a student determine the thesis statement? It is the condensed version of the personal insight or analysis that drove the student to choose the essay question and the essay topic. The thesis statement should allow the reader to know exactly what the essay will say about the student and his experience. It should also lead the reader to the answer of "Why?" It may help students to think of the thesis as the one takeaway point that must come across. This one specific idea is the reason for this essay.

In the essay about Mexico, the thesis statement might be something like, "On my mission trip to Mexico I learned that the more I listened to people's stories about their lives and religious beliefs, the more insight I could gain into my own spiritual goals." The resulting supporting paragraphs could then detail some of these stories and insights. The thesis provides the direction, or "heart," of the entire essay.

Step 4. Show, don't tell—the body of the essay

The main purpose of the essay is to provide personal insight and analysis about the student. The body of the essay includes examples to support this mission. This is quite different from the body of most high school writing assignments, which ask the student to provide persuasive arguments supported by hard facts. College essays require students to *show* what they are writing about, rather than *tell* individual facts about an event or idea. There are three primary ways for students to show rather than tell: description of sensations, action, and dialogue.

- *Description of sensations.* Highlighting sights, sounds, smells, and tastes. Rather than writing about how cold it was, students should conjure images that allow the reader to *feel* what it was like to be that cold.
- *Action.* Elaborating on the actual process. Rather than writing about making the last-second shot, students should give a blow-by-blow account of what led up to making the last-second shot.
- *Dialogue.* Using actual dialogue to give life to the example. Rather than writing that the group leader made her point, use actual quotes to demonstrate how she made her point.

An admissions officer will remain interested in an essay that shows him what happened, rather than just cataloguing events. With continued interest in the essay, there will be continued interest in the student and what he brings to the campus community. By showing the admissions officer their experiences, students also lend credibility to their examples. This furthers the personal insight and analysis necessary for the admissions committee to better understand the student.

When choosing supporting statements and concepts, it is important that these examples move the reader from the description to the analysis of the event or experience. The best examples are those that go beyond describing what happened and demonstrate the impact of the experience on the student. For example, stating,

"I won the race" carries far less meaning than stating, "That victory taught me a great deal about dedication, teamwork, and persistence." It is essential for students to go beyond merely recounting the event and instead attach meaning to the experience.

Step 5. Write a memorable conclusion

After beginning the essay with a powerful opening paragraph and going on to explain the "Why" of the essay, your child should tie everything together with a strong conclusion. Many students look at the conclusion as a way to "tell the reader what has already been told." However, when reading the conclusion, the admissions committee is not looking for a rehash of the essay. They are looking for a final insight—a reaffirmation of the thesis based on the personal examples given in the body of the essay. Students should be reminded that the conclusion is the lasting impression left with the members of the admissions committee.

WARNING! SKIMMER ALERT

Some parents have asked me if admissions officers always read to the end of every essay. I have to say that it is possible that an admissions person will skim when an applicant has not caught his interest at all. If an introduction is very weak, he might not be compelled to pay close attention to the rest of the essay.

Just as it was important to draw the reader into the essay, it is equally important to leave the reader with a final insight that allows the student to stand out from other applicants. Again, the best way to make an impression in writing is to show rather than tell. Ending an essay with, "It felt good to help others" does little to establish the student as memorable. But if the student were to show through description of sensations, action, or dialogue how she came to the same realization, it would make a much more powerful statement about the experience and the student.

It is important to remind students that the conclusion should not introduce any new ideas not addressed in the body of the essay. I have read essays by students who are trying to "save the best for last." They wait until the last sentence or two to introduce a new concept or major epiphany. These students would have a far more convincing essay if they translated that surprise concept or epiphany into a thesis statement and used the body of the essay to explore the impact of that concept or epiphany. Remember that the last line of the essay is the last impression the admissions officer has of the applicant. Leave the college with the best impression possible!

IV. ESSAY WRITING DOS AND DON'TS

By now, you should have a better understanding of the purpose of the essay in the application process. However, it is important to know more about what the writing sample should and should *not* be, so you can help your child avoid some of the most common pitfalls. Remember again that the essay is the only chance the student has to represent himself to the entire admissions committee. If he does not grab the reader's attention with something unique, individual or personal, he has missed a golden opportunity to make an impression. And any mistake can sink the whole ship. This process is too competitive for that, so make sure that your child dots every *i*, crosses every *t*, and follows the guidelines below.

Do: Be Yourself

Encourage your student to represent the most important aspects of his personality, sense of humor, intellect—or whatever he thinks is most important to share with people who do not know him. Remember that admissions committees are building communities through the application process. If they wanted a class filled with identical students, they would not spend the time getting to know students through these essays.

Do: Use Natural Language

A student should be wary of trying to write in a way that is unnatural. While your student needs to stay on topic, the style of writing should be uniquely his. In an attempt to sound more intelligent, some students will resort to using the thesaurus as often as possible. Some students will find uncommon terms and misuse them in an attempt to look creative or intellectual. They should also avoid using language that is not familiar. While there are certain grammar rules students need to follow, they should write in essentially the same manner in which they speak, as long as it is grammatically correct. For instance, don't say "peer" when you mean "friend." Don't say "utilize" when you can say "use." Authenticity counts.

Don't: Try a Gimmick

One way for students to completely bury their identity is to believe a gimmick will help them become memorable. More often than not, the gimmick will backfire and hurt their chances for admission. Over the years, I've read essays that have been written in a tight spiral, forcing me to turn the paper in circles to read the essay. I've had students write their essay backward, so that I had to hold the text up to a mirror to read it. I've also had a student write an essay, attach it to a piece of cardboard, and make it into a puzzle that needed to be assembled in order to read. In each of these cases, the admissions committee opted to deny the student. With the large number of essays admissions officers must read, you don't want to do anything to make their jobs harder.

A gimmick also implies to an admissions committee that a student is a trickster or someone who tries to play outside of the rules—not the type of person they are excited to have join their school community. Gimmicks are annoying. Gimmicks feel like a student's attempt to hide shallowness in a sleek package. Gimmicks simply do not work.

Don't: Exaggerate

Some students think they can fool the admissions committee by exaggerating an accomplishment. Unfortunately, exaggeration usually backfires. If students make claims that are not backed up anywhere else in the application (i.e., recommendation letters, activities charts, transcripts, et cetera), it often sends a red flag to the admissions committee.

Don't: Get Too Personal

Along the same lines, some students will divulge highly personal information (drug addiction, physical abuse, eating disorder, et cetera) and claim they've never shared this information before. If this personal information is still so painful that the student can't share it with anyone but a faceless admissions committee, it might not be the best topic for the college essay.

I believe that some students try this approach for shock value and that fails almost every time. A statement such as, "I have never told another living soul about this . . ." does not add a thing—and probably will hurt a student's chances. When this occurs, some officers believe that the student is lying. Why would a student tell strangers about such a serious and personal issue? If the student truly has nobody else in the world he can tell and the information is true, then the student seems like he needs real help.

Don't: Brag

The essay should not be a place for a student to brag about personal accomplishments. Your child will have the opportunity to highlight accomplishments in the activities section of the application. While a student may choose to write about an activity, honor, award, community service project, or mission trip, the purpose of the essay is to share what he gained from the experience, why it was important, how it changed what he does now, or how it impacts what he wants to do in the future. Your student should take the time to reflect on the importance of the event and should take pride in his accomplishments. The focus of the essay should be an analysis of what happened and what it meant to your child, not, for instance, an overview of why it is impressive to be elected to the National Honor Society.

Don't: Rehash the Activities Chart

Similarly, the essay should not simply repeat information that is found elsewhere on the application. While an essay can, and likely will, mention a significant activity, the emphasis should be a personal experience not detailed in the application materials. If your student has already documented a large amount of time to a sport, committee, or other activity, the essay should explore areas that allow the admissions committee to see another side of the student. For instance, if your daughter is a soccer star and this fact appears in multiple places in the application, she might choose to write an essay that takes place at a soccer tournament, but the essay should focus on a life lesson she learned at the tournament (such as leadership, friendship, or cultural sensitivity) using the sport as the backdrop and not the focus. This is a smart way to incorporate an application theme of soccer without sounding too one-dimensional. She can use the soccer experience as a way to show a particular element of her personality.

Don't: Give Excuses

If your student has not performed to the level he would have liked in high school, the essay is not the place to make excuses. If there is an event, an illness, or an unexplained circumstance that had a significant impact on the student's academic performance, and your student can analyze the impact of the situation on her overall performance, then it may be worth exploring for an essay topic. That being said, unless the essay can pinpoint the cause of the problem and explain how the student has overcome the problem, the student will be doing himself a disservice by writing an essay about poor performance. Simply saying that he lacked motivation, did not realize the importance of high school classes, or did not like a specific subject will not impress an admissions committee. Honesty is important, but your child should not "market" his weaknesses by making them the focus of an essay.

Do: Give a Slice of Life, Not the Whole Story

Perhaps the hardest thing for students to realize about the college essay is that it is *not* their life story in five hundred words or less. In my experience, students try to give a complete picture of who they are, where they've come from, and what they want to do—all in a few hundred words! While any admissions committee would like to have the flexibility and time to read complete histories of each and every student, the simple truth is, there is not enough time. Students must understand, that the college essay is the best way for an admission committee to know *something* about them, but it cannot be the vehicle to know *everything* about them.

Don't: Pick a Poor or Overused Topic

Perhaps the two most overused essay topics are the "trip" essays and the "sports/sports injury" essays. These topics set students up to give empty descriptions of common activities done by almost every student applying to a college or university. The quality of the description may be flawless, but often the essays lack the reflection and meaning necessary to have an impact on the admissions committee. Trip essays are usually written in beautiful, colorful language. Students will describe the trip they took to an impoverished town in Mexico, the beauty of the countryside, the friendliness of the townspeople, or the realization of how little the townspeople have in comparison to what they have. What is missing is the analysis of what all of these realizations mean. Students need to address why this was a meaningful experience and what it has meant to how they now approach life as a result. Did it change their outlook? Do they have a newfound commitment to helping those less fortunate? Will they seek out ways to continue similar activities once they are on campus?

The sports and sports injury essays are even more common than the trip essays, and they lure students into the same trap. In graphic detail, students will describe the "pop!" they heard in their knee, the gasp of the crowd as they fell to the field or the court, and their feelings of despair thinking they would never play [insert sport here] again. They might explore the feelings of exhilaration as they dribbled down the court for one last-second shot, the roar of the crowd as time expired, and the intense feelings experienced, regardless of whether the ball makes it through the basket. All of this description means nothing without analysis of its importance, the impact it had, or the lasting effects of the injury or game. Did it give the student confidence that he applied elsewhere in his life? Did losing the big game change his priorities? Did an experience in sports lead to mentoring younger kids trying the same game?

It is important for the essay writer to use the trip, sport, or injury only as backdrop to set up the analysis of why the experience was meaningful.

Don't: Pick a Topic Out of a Book

You may have noticed that there are no sample essays in this chapter, and only simple examples of some of the tools and techniques used in creating a strong college essay. This is deliberate: every student will—and should—approach essay writing differently. What works for one student may not work for another. Also, it is far too easy to look at an example that is deemed "strong" and try to mimic it.

When I worked at Indiana University, essays were not required; however, many students would include an essay to show their writing proficiency. One year, every other essay had something to do with a genie appearing out of a college viewbook. The genie would grant the student three wishes but ultimately ended up directing the student to Indiana University. As it turned out, there was a guidebook in essay writing that used a similar essay as an example of a strong essay. Rather than taking note of the components that made the essay strong, students mimicked the essay and submitted it as an original idea. Unfortunately, that original idea was less than original and did not help the admissions committee to know the students.

Do: Write and Edit Your Own Essay

Because maintaining the student's voice is so critical to the success of a powerful essay, no matter how well someone knows the student, another person cannot accurately depict the student's thoughts and feelings. Avoid, at all cost, having someone help rewrite or redraft the essay, because it will end up sounding false and disconnected. It is also important to note that when a student asks for feedback on an essay, he should not just take the comments or suggestions and add them word-for-word into the essay. If the student randomly inserts someone else's thoughts, he will lose his own voice. Instead, encourage your child to restate any helpful suggestions in his own words, using his own vocabulary and writing style.

Do: Write a New Essay for Every New Essay Question

As much work as the essay is, it is an important statement about the student for the admissions committee. Just as every student in the applicant pool is unique, so is every institution to which a student applies. Students should tailor their essays to the individual schools on their list. It is important that the student recognize that different schools are looking for different things in the essay. As such, students should be starting fresh with each new essay question to ensure they are answering the "Why?" for that specific school. This means carefully reading the essay question and responding—not "shoehorning" an essay to fit a different question. The only time you can ever reuse an essay is for the questions on the Common Application. Even then, depending on the topic, the essay may need to be adjusted for each individual school, perhaps to talk about a specific major or activity the student plans to pursue at that school.

V. EDITING AND REVISING

Students should use the tools listed in this chapter to generate the first draft, but the writing process does not end there. Students should complete the first draft, set it aside for a day or two, and then come back to it with a clear head to make updates and corrections. An essay is never as strong after the first draft as it will be after several revisions.

While both spell-check and grammar-check are helpful tools, they are not failsafe. In fact, spell-check actually only picks out words that are misspelled, not misused. In my years of reviewing college essays, I have encountered the football *couch* and have learned that there are way too many candy *strippers*. It is also amazing to me how many students are on the honor *role*. While these silly mistakes do provide some comic relief for the admissions committee members, it is not likely to help a student's chances for admission.

As a parent, you can help your child edit and revise. This proofreading goes beyond checking for spelling and grammar errors. Proofreading means looking for factual errors, making sure that the correct school name is in the appropriate essay, and that the correct supplementary materials are with the appropriate application. It means taking time to ensure all of the student's hard work gets to the right place, at the right time, with the appropriate materials. At some schools, guidance counselors and teachers will agree to proofread and offer suggestions on college essays as well.

In some cases, the best person to give feedback is a child's close friend. A peer review will allow the student to receive honest feedback from someone who is going through the same process at the same time. The student's friend should be able to read through the essay and say, "That sounds just like you!" If the reaction is anything else, the student may want to revise the essay to find a voice more closely aligned with his personality.

Here are some additional suggestions for editing, proofreading, and revising.

- Read the essay backward. This provides the chance to see words that might be used incorrectly that the eye glosses over (e.g., *there* instead of *their*.)

- Compare the final essay to the original outline to make sure all of the points are there and the essay flows logically. Check that all of the points in the body support the thesis statement.
- Fact-check carefully. If the essay references any proper names of people, places, or institutions, triple check the spelling, capitalization, and punctuation. Fact-check the consistency of the student's personal references as well. If the student lists herself as president of the student council in her activities chart, she should also be president in the essay if it mentions that position.

This chapter provided some tools to help your student craft a personal and analytical essay, as well as given you a better understanding of why colleges and universities ask students to spend so much time on the essay. Essay writing does not need to be the most stressful and feared portion of the college application process. It is an opportunity for your child to shine.

CHAPTER 7

ACTIVITIES

Expert Coach: Jennifer Duran,
Former Admissions Officer, Columbia University

In the same way the academic transcript is intended to capture an applicant's academic accomplishments, the activities chart functions as a personal profile, or résumé, detailing and documenting how a student used his free time during the high school years. This includes school-based extracurriculars, community activities, other clubs and organizations. Generally, one interest or activity is not considered any better than another. Rather, it is how far a student takes an interest and how well it is described on the application that really matters.

It may seem that students with a stronger activity profile have "the right stuff" to make their applications shine. But often students believe that their activities will be obvious to admissions officers, so they spend little time on the activity component of their applications. This is a big mistake. The truth is that *how* your child presents his list of activities on the college application can be just as important as the activities themselves. Filling in the activities chart is an art.

RULES TO REMEMBER IN THIS CHAPTER

- **Colleges are impressed by quality, not quantity.** While the emphasis of this chapter is indeed to make you aware that your child's activities matter and are an important part of the process, the caution is that he should not overextend himself. Yes, activities are important, but it is meaningful and sustained involvement that colleges seek—not the longest list.
- **Be strategic about the activities chart.** Students need to think carefully about both what should be included and how to prioritize the information. They should prioritize the activities that have been most important to them, have offered the greatest challenge or level of growth, or those to which they have devoted the greatest amount of time. Students should also be sure that the activities chart supports the overall application theme.
- **Be smart about supplemental submissions.** Understand the merit and strategy for supplemental submissions including résumés, portfolios, audition tapes, CDs, athletics letters, and formal explanations of unique circumstances. This can be a great strategy (and is often required for arts programs), but submitting irrelevant or unimpressive supplemental materials can hurt an application. Ask yourself: Is this truly worth submitting? Will a nonbiased party see this as useful and insightful information? If not, don't include it.

I. WHY ACTIVITIES MATTER

As you have read in previous chapters, students don't get admitted on grades alone: it is the combination of academics and extracurricular activities that, more than likely, will impress an admissions committee enough to offer the student a spot in their school's community. This is especially true at the most competitive colleges. Extracurricular involvement is vital to distinguish one applicant from another in the admissions process. With a strong activity profile, students rise above the pool as unique individuals with distinct and diverse abilities and skills. The more substantial the involvement, combined with the levels of proficiency and leadership of the applicant, the more compelling the student becomes.

Since the application activities chart asks for information about the years of a student's participation in each activity, let's briefly review what admissions officers like to see, year by year.

Freshmen and Sophomores

Early in their high school career prospective applicants should try to sample different clubs and organizations, making a concerted effort to decide which are most interesting. This is definitely a time for students to explore and be part of several organizations. Students should try to decide which activities to follow and pursue more seriously into their junior and senior years.

Clearly, the earlier your student starts, the more opportunity there is to modify activities in an effort to build a strong college application theme. As your child's interests begin to surface, he can further pursue activities and leadership positions that support that particular interest. For instance, a girl who shows an interest in astronomy may decide to pursue a part-time job at a planetarium or an internship at an observatory as opposed to competing for a leadership position in the Key Club. Or, a boy who loves his freshman-year involvement in a community impact organization might find that he cares most about the America Reads program. He could then become more involved in that organization and perhaps begin a chapter at his school, rather than spending time in a variety of other volunteer projects related to other causes.

Juniors and Seniors

As students move into junior year, they should begin to concentrate more on identifying the hobbies and pursuits that are of most significance—a passion, if it exists. Plans for summer programs or internships should also be well under way. Students should assess their profiles and position themselves to pursue leadership roles in organizations.

Families sometimes have the false expectation that a student can identify and fulfill a passion starting in the summer of senior year. In most cases, the student falls short because of time. How much can a student realistically do and feel in a three-to six-month period? The best involvement starts early and evolves over the student's high school career.

DON'T PANIC: IS THERE ANYTHING WE CAN DO IF MY CHILD DIDN'T START EARLY?

An eleventh grader still has time to become meaningfully involved in extracurricular activity, volunteer effort, or work experience if he really wants to. A junior can become involved in something meaningful and even become a leader by senior year.

For a senior, it is a lot tougher to build a meaningful activities profile in just a few months. The problem is that there is no real opportunity for the student to explore a passion or demonstrate real progress. Short-term intensity can work in rare instances, such as a student who spends a three-week December vacation working on a volunteer project. This type of last-minute attempt can work if it ties with the student's application theme, or with another important aspect of the student's application, such as his best academic subject. Unfortunately, if this is done in isolation, it is probably going to look like a Band-Aid—an ineffective one.

Depth versus Breadth

The most common question I hear from parents regarding activities is, "How involved should my child be?" There is no definitive answer to this question, and there are certainly many factors to consider when determining how involved a student can be given a student's academic schedule, activities offered at the school, and a student's commute, among other things. While these factors are indeed important in determining the amount of time a student has for extracurricular activities, there is no predetermined number of hours of involvement that guarantees admission to college.

As a general rule, a student with significant involvement in a limited number of activities is more attractive to an admissions committee than a student who is involved in many activities and demonstrates no depth in his pursuits. In other words, Jimmy's activities—which include three years as member of the Spanish club and one year as vice president, first violin in the orchestra, and a two-year stint as a cashier at the local grocery store—are more appealing to an admissions committee than Karen's pursuits, which include a year as a member of the Spanish club, a year in the band, a year playing on the JV field hockey team, and four months working at the local pharmacy. Jimmy's activities, while fewer in number, show commitment. His position as vice president of the Spanish club speaks to his dedication to the club and his growing leadership skills. Jimmy's time as first violin speaks to his discipline and his mastery. And then there are his two years at the grocery store, which admissions professionals see as an opportunity that teaches him responsibility and maturity.

Overall, Jimmy's activities are a clear indicator of his growth, therefore making him more appealing to colleges and universities. His involvement shows real depth over time, and as such, he is able to rise into positions of leadership. Karen, on the other hand, while demonstrating a plethora of interests, appears to be noncommittal in her pursuits. She tries things out for a year at a time and is never able to rise to the helm of a group or team. In the end, this lack of focus and dedication could make other candidates more appealing. Candidates with a focus are easier for admissions officers to present to their colleagues when they are describing them as potential members of the school community: "This is the kid who will probably major in Spanish and will be a serious member of our orchestra."

DON'T PANIC! WHAT IF MY CHILD'S ACTIVITIES ARE NOT FOCUSED?

If your child is more like Karen than Jimmy, the best strategy is to look for commonalities in the random activities and prioritize activities at the top of the list that can work together as a theme. Many times there are subtle commonalities among activities. For instance, a student who plays on two sports teams, participates in the yearbook committee, and spent a year cheerleading might create a theme about being involved in student activities. If her essays, recommendations, and interview all support this type of theme, then the seemingly unconnected activities make much more sense and look more impressive to an admissions officer. Now this is "the girl who will participate in lots of activities, wear the college sweatshirt everywhere, probably join a sorority, and be a resident adviser her senior year."

II. THE ART OF COMPLETING THE ACTIVITIES CHART

The activities chart is a compilation of the student's extracurricular activities and involvement outside the classroom. There are many different categories and areas that are included as part of this chart, including any pursuit that is not directly connected to academic classes. If a student is involved in high school clubs and athletic teams, those should also appear on the chart. Similarly, any community organizations and summer programs should be listed here as well. Below we have reproduced an activities chart taken from the Common Application. Schools that do not accept the Common Application are likely to ask students to fill out a similar chart.

EXTRACURRICULAR, PERSONAL, AND VOLUNTEER ACTIVITIES (including summer)

Please list your **principal** extracurricular, community, and family activities and hobbies **in the order of their interest to you.** Include specific events and/or major accomplishments such as musical instrument played, varsity letters earned, etc. Check (✓) in the right column those activities you hope to pursue in college. **To allow us to focus on the highlights of your activities, please complete this section even if you plan to send a résumé.**

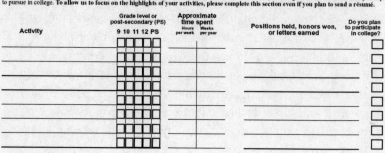

The information included in this part of the application should list the type of activity, the duration of involvement, and whether the student held any positions of leadership within the organization. Favorite hobbies and clubs should be listed first and least favorite should go last. Students should resist that desire to list activities in chronological order. The emphasis should be on the most significant and meaningful pursuits, not documenting every moment of free time in his high school career.

Not only does the chart show the level and amount of participation, it also tells a story about the student's character and maturity. These learning experiences help the applicant to develop and cultivate unique characteristics, leadership skills, talents, and traits that are easily observed through his pursuits. Admissions professionals know that the student holding leadership responsibilities in a club or increasing responsibilities at a volunteer school job is apt to be more mature and responsible. Also, this student tends to be more advanced in developing social and professional skills. He is more independent and is more at ease in social situations (including college interviews). And, he might even experience less anxiety about leaving home for college.

NEW RULE OF COLLEGE ADMISSIONS: EVERY LINE AND BOX COUNTS

The most common mistake that students make on the activities chart is to "blow off" the details. Here is some insight into why every line and box matter to admissions officers:

- **Activity List:** Make sure the activities are listed in order of preference to the student. This is how the admissions officer determines what is most important to the student.
- **Years of Participation and Approximate Time Spent:** Be careful not to overestimate or underestimate. These answers indicate how dedicated the student is to various activities. It also shows honesty—admissions officers are skeptical when a student says he spends twenty hours a week on six different clubs and sports teams!
- **Positions Held, Honors Won, or Letters Earned:** This is extremely important and details matter. Was a student a member of a committee or the elected president? Did he move up the ranks from JV to varsity? This category gives admissions officers information about the student's level of motivation, self-confidence (did he run for office?), reputation among peers, teachers, and community members, and his level of maturity.
- **Do You Plan to Participate in College?** Not all applications ask this question, but the Common Application does. When in doubt, it's a good idea for the student to check off this box if the school offers a similar activity. Do not encourage your child to lie, but checking this box shows further commitment to a student's interests and a desire to become an involved member of the college community.

In the end, the activities chart is a sales pitch for the student. Remind your child not to hold back any impressive information that will help his admissions chances.

Supporting the Application Theme

A student's chart is most effective when it supports the overall application theme. Again, the theme should inform how the student's candidacy is presented and what recurrent ideas are highlighted in the application. Colleges and universities go to great lengths to recruit and admit students who represent a variety of interests and talents. They set about recruiting students representing different geographic regions, ethnic backgrounds, academic interests, extracurricular profiles, and so on. They devote time to finding qualified athletes, scientists, and artists.

To that end, schools have to consider a student's activities, involvement, and interests in shaping a class that represents the diversity and all the possibilities of their applicant pool. If an applicant is a budding scientist looking to pursue a major in biochemical engineering, his activities should highlight any Westinghouse or Intel research projects he might be running. It should also include any research positions or science club participation. All the activities and involvement should begin to create the profile of a serious scientist and researcher, thus making it easier for an admissions committee to decide what place that particular applicant occupies in the incoming class. Similarly, the student who is positioning herself as a future filmmaker proves her value by her leadership role in the school film club and an internship at a local movie production company. The consistent and recurring themes in these examples help a student stand out. An activities chart supports the theme by providing a clear-cut list of activities, as well as showing a student's continued commitment over time.

Prioritize Carefully

The task of choosing and prioritizing the information included on the activities chart may seem daunting, but it is the most crucial part of the process. Here are the two tasks at hand:

1. **Select which activities to include.** The amount of included information is limited and not all activities may be included, so a student must consider some important things.

Generally speaking, activities that engage a student for an hour or more a week, consistently throughout the course of a semester, should be included in any chart.

2. **Rank the activities.** Once the student has listed the activities to which he devoted most of his time, he will need to rank the ones that are most important. Remember that the chart should emphasize the most significant and meaningful pursuits. Even those that do make the top of the list should be activities about which the student is passionate. Ideally, the student has also spent the most time on the activities he finds most meaningful. Perhaps the student holds the position of rep-at-large in student government or maybe he was a founding member of the ballroom dancing club. Perhaps he spent more than ten hours a week at the America Reads Program, the activity to which he dedicated most of his time. Keep in mind that some activities may not make the final list, as they may not be as significant as other activities higher up on the list.

It may be challenging for students to compile the activities chart. Sometimes they will overlook a commitment because it seems unimportant or not noteworthy. As a parent, you can help your child brainstorm and prioritize. Initially, ask your child to write down any activities in the categories below, and then have him "rank" the categories and activities in order of importance. Here is a list of the most common categories, including examples and strategic guidelines to help you guide your student. Note that your child may not have any activities in certain categories, which is fine.

School Activities and Clubs

- Examples: student government, debate team, school newspaper, yearbook, science club, homecoming committee, chess theater, choir.
- Strategy: Remember that the best activities charts tivities that relate to the student's application theme.

Sports

- Examples: swimming, football, soccer, squash, fencing, tennis, cross-country, crew, cycling, equestrian, baseball, softball.
- Strategy: Include school-related sports and local, regional, or national participation. A personal athletic hobby can be included if it takes a significant amount of the student's time, but this is not as impressive as an organized athletic activity. If the student goes to a gym three times a week, that is not enough. But, if student goes to a gym three times a week and competes in bodybuilding weight lifting competitions, that should be included.

DON'T PANIC! WHAT IF MY CHILD PLAYED ON A SPORTS TEAM AND THEN QUIT?

If your child quit a sports team after a year or two, should he still include it on the activities chart? It depends. If your child has many other activities to list, then I would recommend leaving it off. If your child does not have a long list of activities, then I would advise including the fact that he tried the sport. Two years of football is not worthless, but it may not make the list for someone with many other activities to mention.

Community Service and Volunteering

- Examples: tutoring, hospital volunteering, religious organizations, gathering sponsors and participating in a bike-a-thon.
- Strategy: If your child has participated in a variety of volunteer efforts, he may choose to list "community service—urban programs" or "community service—work with children" instead of each small activity. This is a good strategy for a student who has participated in many one-off events but has not been consistently involved with one particular volunteer organization. If the area in which your child volunteers relates to his theme (such as music, children, communication, agriculture, animals, et cetera), then all the better.

Work Experience

- Examples: store clerk, law firm internship, Little League coach, camp counselor, babysitter, office receptionist.
- Strategy: It's best to prioritize work experience that fits with a student's theme. Work experience, even if it is unpaid, can be a good strategy for students without a lot of school-related activities to list. It shows maturity and responsibility.

Summer Programs

- Examples: academic enrichment programs, volunteer programs.
- Strategy: Prioritize summer programs that fit with the application theme.

Hobbies

- Examples: playing piano, coin collecting, hiking, astronomy.
- Strategy: There are no "good" or "bad" hobbies. Admissions officers are looking for passion and sustained commitment. If a skill has developed through a hobby, then your child should highlight it. However, be sure the hobby does not raise questions. For instance, if piano is a student's hobby, he plays by himself, never enters competitions, doesn't participate in music classes at school, or teach piano lessons in the summer, admissions officers might wonder why not. Only include a hobby if it shows commitment and real interest.

Travel

- Examples: domestic travel, international travel, sailing trips, camping.
- Strategy: Taking a family trip is not impressive in itself, but this can make a student appear more worldly. Trips that involve home stays, community service, language immersion, or cultural exchange with other teenagers are better. Again, travel is best if it supports an overall theme.

Honors and Awards

- Examples: local scholarships, academic awards, community service honors.

- Strategy: While there is space on the activities chart for awards related to activities, it is also recommended to list additional honors.

Independent Ventures

- Examples: started an after-school program to teach grade school students how to use computers, organized an antique car show, revived the town snack bar.
- Strategy: These types of projects can be very impressive and should not be overlooked. Ventures that support a student's application theme are, of course, the most impressive.

Presentation

A vast majority of colleges request a student's activities in chart form, although there are a few schools that request their own specific format. Some will simply ask students to detail their time in a format similar to a work history résumé. As in a chart, the student's interests and involvement should be compiled in a format that is easy to follow and will highlight the student's participation by focusing on the most significant activities. In all cases, the student should fill out the chart that is provided—even if the student does not feel the format is particularly helpful in stating his case.

DON'T PANIC! WHAT IF MY CHILD RUNS OUT OF ROOM ON THE CHART?

Although I believe students should try to prioritize their activities to fit in the chart provided on the application, it can be okay to use an additional sheet of paper. Many schools state on the application that this is acceptable. In attaching the additional sheet, do try to keep the same format so it is easy for the admissions officer to follow.

However, do not add an extra sheet of paper just for the sake of doing so. A few tough admissions officers may feel annoyed if the extra sheet feels superfluous. Only include an extra sheet of paper if the number of activities requires it.

III. TO SUBMIT OR NOT TO SUBMIT: SUPPLEMENTAL INFORMATION

I find that most parents believe that more is better. "Why not send in a graphic design portfolio or a solo CD?" Contrary to popular belief, most students do not benefit from supplemental submissions. In this section I will outline the three most common types of extra information sent by applicants and discuss ways to make a good decision about when it is appropriate to send additional information.

WARNING! DON'T FORGET

If your child does choose to submit supplemental information, be sure all material displays your child's contact information. With hundreds of tapes, videos, papers, and files, things can get lost in the shuffle.

Résumé

Most applications provide ample space for activities, employment, volunteerism, and a course outline. Students seem to believe that if they create a résumé, they no longer need to worry about fitting their experiences into the format the college application provides, as some students may find it limiting. Nothing could be further from the truth.

On the other hand, some students do an excellent job filling out the application. They use the résumé so admissions can develop a deep level of understanding about a particular group of activities. If a student has the type of background where in-depth information will show positively, a résumé can help. For instance, a résumé would be appropriate for a student with exceptional talent, such as a world-class musician or a national champion figure skater.

Portfolios, Auditions, CDs, DVDs

When applicants are considering a specialized art program in college, they will often be asked to submit a portfolio. Applicants who demonstrate a strong inclination for the arts and have amassed credentials in their area of interest should be pleased to support their accomplishments with documents of their achievement. When the student is a performer, an audition may be required.

When there are no portfolio or audition requirements and the student has obvious talent, he can still submit performances; awards; commendations; evidence of lead roles in orchestras and choruses, plays, and movies; a DVD with video clips from performances or a CD with audio clips. Students with significant achievements in the visual arts can compile a portfolio with pictures or slides that highlight and visually depict the student's works. Any distinctions for the pieces should also be noted. Any noteworthy newspaper or magazine articles should accompany these additional materials.

Students should check with the admissions office to see how the information should best be presented when it accompanies the application. This is important, as the applicant will want to submit as much information as possible—but not too much—to support the application. Follow the specific guidelines of each school to make sure your child is submitting in the appropriate way.

WARNING! GET A SECOND OPINION

Parents are usually not the best judges of how talented a child really is. Before your student makes a submission to support a talent, make sure that a knowledgeable critic assures you that his talent is evident in the submission. Poor portfolios and musical tapes can hurt a student's claim that he will be a key contributor to an arts program.

Athletics

The accomplished student athlete is in a unique position: he will present his credentials to the admissions committee for consideration and he can also appeal to coaches for additional support. As part of recruiting efforts, coaches can begin contacting students July 1 prior to their senior year. Before then, their contact with students may be limited. Even during the recruitment process, their contact with students is strictly governed by National Collegiate Athletic Association (NCAA) rules.

However, there are no rules that prohibit or preclude the student from initiating contact with the coach. In fact, it may be beneficial for a student to get his name on the radar by writing letters to specific colleges and providing athletic departments with stats, video clips, and articles about his success. This should be done sometime during junior year to increase the chances that he will be contacted during the senior year recruitment cycle. The idea here would be very similar to, and consistent with, the above guidelines for submission of portfolios and other supplemental credentials.

Here is an example of a note a student might write to a college athletic coach during the summer of her junior year. This note was provided by Christine Kelley, a former admissions officer from Harvard University.

May 31, 2005

Coach Jane Smith
1234 College Street
State University
Collegeville, US 12345

Dear Coach Smith,

I am writing to introduce myself as a hopeful hockey recruit.

I will be a senior at Memorial High School in the fall and a four-year member of the varsity hockey team. I am also the leading scorer for our team, the Wildcats. I am an honors student with a 3.0 average and hope to major in psychology in college.

I am a longtime fan of the State University Bears and would like to learn more about your program and how I might fit in with your team in the future. I have enclosed a copy of my résumé, which lists my statistics in more detail. I would welcome the opportunity to talk with you and learn more about State hockey.

Thank you for your time.

Sincerely,

Victoria Corcoran

Formal Explanations

For the most part, a student presents himself through academics, activities, interviews, essays, and test scores. There are rare cases when admissions would appreciate a more in-depth understanding of something that could be looked at as a negative. Examples that come to mind are: grade decline, disciplinary issues, and unfortunate circumstances. A formal explanation about "low test scores" is in most instances ineffective. Admissions officers understand that some students do not test well.

A student needs to have a good reason that is real and true to effectively explain away a problem. For example, a parent's death can explain a poor grade on a final exam. Similarly, a teacher who is acting in an inappropriate way and has since been terminated for his behavior can account for a disciplinary problem that is on a record. In these unique circumstances, applicants are encouraged to submit an explanation separate from the activities chart. As explained in chapter 1, such issues are best explained by the student's guidance counselor. When parents and students try to make excuses, admissions officers can be skeptical. A third-party explanation is much more credible, so talk to your child's guidance counselor if you feel any issue needs to be explained.

The activities chart is one way to highlight a student's strengths aside from traditional classroom achievement. It should support the application theme and offer further insight into a student's interests, maturity, and dedication.

CHAPTER 8

LETTERS OF RECOMMENDATION

Expert Coach: Julia Jones,
Former Admissions Officer, Brandeis University

Letters of recommendation are the only pieces of information in a college application not created or submitted directly by the applicant. But, fear not! Proactive students and parents can take several steps to secure positive recommendation letters that enhance an application.

In many cases, recommendations neither help nor hurt an applicant. Letters generally come in above average, but not amazing—and that is what we admissions officers tend to expect. Sometimes, however, a recommendation is particularly special, and that moves an applicant out of "maybe" and into "admit." Conversely, every once in a while, a recommendation can cause a rejection. I have read letters from people who obviously do not know the applicant well at all, which implies that the student has not distinguished himself at his high school. Even worse, letters sometimes contradict information that the student provided.

In this chapter, we will look at ways to make your child's recommendations among the special ones. It takes planning, extra effort, and, as always, a strong strategy. Ultimately, recommendations serve as another tool that can help distinguish students in the application process. Recommendations from a guidance counselor or a well-chosen and well-prepared teacher can highlight what makes your child a unique, interesting, and exciting applicant. Like personal statements, excellent recommendations can make your child "come alive" to an admissions committee in a way that no transcript ever could.

RULES TO REMEMBER IN THIS CHAPTER

- **Understand the positive role recommendations can play in the application process.** A strong letter of recommendation corroborates and expands on information from a student's transcript, supports his application theme, and shows admissions officers how that student would fit into the college's community.
- **Choose recommendation writers carefully.** Help your child determine the best recommenders by looking at the teachers he knows best, likes best, and has shared experiences with outside the classroom.
- **Prepare your child's recommenders.** While your child can't write the recommendation letter himself, he can provide teachers with sufficient information to ensure the recommendation is most helpful and in sync with his overall application theme. Your child should tell the recommender, in writing, the qualities he hopes to highlight in his application. This encourages the writer to elaborate on those traits or areas, thus strengthening your child's theme—and chances of admission.
- **Carefully consider additional recommendations.** You may find there are other people in your student's life who could provide a different and unique perspective to an admissions committee. Colleges are not interested in reading much more than what they request, so only include additional letters if they truly offer illuminating opinions and perspectives not otherwise offered by the guidance counselor or teachers.

I. THE ROLE OF RECOMMENDATIONS

While maybe not the most important element of a students' application, a strong letter of recommendation can be an extremely valuable component, as it can illustrate how a student stands out from his peers. Taken separately—the transcript, GPA, grades, SATs, résumé, essay, interview, and yes, the recommendations—don't mean much, but connect them together, and you start to get a picture of a complete student: his strengths and weaknesses, interests and passions, character traits and qualities. The components are different in nature: some are factual and objective, like grades and SATs. Other components—personal essays and the recommendations—are more subjective and provide the nuances that put the numbers into the appropriate context. A strong letter of recommendation both supports and expands on information from the transcript, adding more detail to the impression of a student conveyed in his application.

NEW RULE OF COLLEGE ADMISSIONS: INCREASED COMPETITION MEANS THAT EVERYTHING MATTERS MORE

As the college admissions game has become increasingly competitive, students need to find as many ways as possible to distinguish themselves. A fabulous recommendation letter can do just that. Whereas in the past students might not have paid as much attention to the process of asking teachers for letters, kids today can no longer afford to be lax about anything that affects their applications. As you will see in this chapter, your child needs to spend time deciding whom to ask, preparing the teacher to write the recommendation, and making sure everything is submitted on time.

Always remember that admissions officers are not only looking for good students in their classrooms; they're looking for students who are going to be great roommates, positive forces in the residence halls. They want students who will enhance the university student life. Letters of recommendation can help paint a picture of your child as a whole person—academically and socially—that will help an admissions committee see your child as a living, breathing member of their college community.

Now let's look at what kinds of recommendations are required.

Guidance Counselor Recommendations

Virtually all schools require a recommendation from the student's guidance counselor. Unlike the teacher recommendations, here the student doesn't get to choose who writes the letter. In most cases, a student's guidance counselor is assigned in ninth grade and never changes.

The important thing for students and parents to recognize is that colleges are less concerned with the guidance counselor recommendation, because it's rarely particularly revealing. That said, a recommendation from a counselor that is full of depth and insight is a welcome surprise, a bonus. What this means is that, if your child has the opportunity to get to know his guidance counselor, beyond just the precursory meeting every term, it is a benefit and worth the effort.

Your child might schedule a separate "get-to-know-you" meeting with his guidance counselor, ideally sophomore or junior year. The meeting should essentially be a chat, where your child can share a bit about his interests, classes, activities, and potential future goals so the guidance counselor gets to know him apart from other students. This type of meeting may prove difficult because counselors are quite busy, but the extra effort will generally be appreciated and will serve your student well. The truth is that counselors are usually all too familiar with "problem" kids, and are also aware of the "stars," so this is an important strategy if your child is quiet or tends to fall to the middle of the academic pack. A little extra effort from your child with a guidance counselor now can pay off in an above-average recommendation letter from that counselor later. If your child is already a senior, he can make an extra effort to be prepared and engaging during required meetings with the guidance counselor about college. No matter what, be sure to talk to your child about the importance of making a positive impression.

DON'T PANIC! WHAT IF MY CHILD'S HIGH SCHOOL IS LARGE AND THE GUIDANCE COUNSELORS EACH HAVE TOO MANY STUDENTS TO GIVE EACH ONE ADEQUATE ATTENTION?

Rest assured that admissions officers are aware of the differences in high schools, and of the huge differences in the counselor caseloads at various high schools. They will regard the counselor recommendation accordingly, in the context of the individual high school.

The Common Application school report form, which is the common form for the guidance counselor recommendation, asks the question, "How long have you known the applicant, and in what context?" When I was an admissions officer reading applications, it was the first item on the form I reviewed; it gave me the right perspective, whether the recommendation was from a counselor who works with more than five hundred students or only fifty. I've read some recommendations that were only a sentence or two in length, and others that were a couple of pages.

Teacher Recommendations

Most selective schools require two teacher recommendations. Some schools are more particular, such as Trinity College, in Hartford, Connecticut, which strongly recommends that one of the recommendations is from an eleventh grade English or history teacher, so that Trinity's admissions officers can evaluate a student's writing ability. And some may require only one recommendation, or even none, keeping the submission of recommendations optional. Bottom line: two solid, strong teacher recommendations will cover most students for most college applications.

By and large, it's the teacher recommendations that will provide the real insight into a student—more than the guidance counselor recommendation. Think about it: Who could be in a better position to describe your child than someone who's seen him every day in class and witnessed his progress, growth, and development as a student?

II. FIVE STEPS TO SECURING WINNING RECOMMENDATION LETTERS

While it's true that students cannot write their recommendations themselves, there are steps that any student should take to ensure that teachers and guidance counselors are writing engaging, pertinent, and winning letters. Your job as the parent is to help monitor this process.

Step 1. Advise your child to build and maintain relationships
You are likely already aware of the relationships your child has with his teachers and guidance counselor. These relationships take on a new significance when it comes to the process of requesting letters of recommendation. In general, the more effort a student has dedicated throughout high school into being an engaged, curious, and interactive student, the stronger the recommendations will be.

The most important advice here is to begin early. Students must take active steps to get teachers to notice them, to really know and appreciate who they are as people and not just test takers and homework doers. The key is to show initiative, curiosity, and a passion for learning. Encourage your child from the very start (ninth grade, if possible) to build strong teacher-student relationships in high school—to speak up in class, seek out a teacher's help and assistance after class, or, if assistance isn't necessary, have him offer to help others. These are inevitably the kinds of comments and stories that teachers will include in their letters of recommendations—and they are precisely the qualities that college professors and, consequently, admissions committees, are looking for.

The benefits and value of becoming a more engaged and involved student go far beyond just the acquisition of a good recommendation. Strong teacher relationships and active class participation make for a much more fulfilling educational experience for your child in high school and will prepare him for the academic and intellectual expectations of whatever college he attends.

DON'T PANIC: IS IT TOO LATE IF MY CHILD IS A SENIOR AND HASN'T BEEN A VERY ENGAGED STUDENT?

What can a first-semester senior year do to make up for a lack of teacher relationships? As long as the desire to improve is genuine, it is never too late for your child to become a more engaged student with stronger connections to teachers. Here are some pointers to recommend to your child.

- **Prepare and participate.** Even if your child has been less than engaged or even unprepared, teachers always respect preparation and effort. Encourage your child to study, take part in class discussions, and even request extra credit assignments.
- **Come to a review sessions for a test.** Again, any show of effort is appreciated by teachers. Attending a review session shows commitment and desire to improve and perform well.
- **Chat after class.** Even though the personal relationship will not be there, your child can still make an attempt to forge a connection beyond just sitting in class. This comes easier

to some kids than others, so talk to your child about whether this would be comfortable. It's best to make the most effort with a teacher the child already likes or the teacher of a subject your child really enjoys.

Step 2. Help your child assess which teachers are likely to write the best recommendations

Now the real fun begins. Which two teachers will write the best recommendation for your child? Just because your daughter loved her eleventh-grade math teacher doesn't mean the feeling is mutual, that the teacher knows your child better than any other in the class, or that she is the best qualified person to represent your daughter's strengths as a student and community member. Thinking carefully about how well, and through what context, the teacher knows the student is just one of the several criteria that leads students to making the best possible choices about teacher recommenders.

When your child chooses the teacher for his recommendations, he should worry less about what subject the teacher has taught. Some students worry that it has to be from a teacher in the subject of their intended major or that it has to be their strongest subject. While it often is the case, because obviously your child is going to be most engaged in his favorite subject, the recommendation doesn't *have* to come from the teacher of that subject. Students also shouldn't worry too much about the grade they received in the course. Some of the best recommendations I have ever read have been from teachers in subjects where the student really struggled and was not top of the class. These recommendations stood out for the admissions committee because they showed, through examples, the student's perseverance, initiative, and hard work. It's easy for most of us to excel and work hard in subjects that we enjoy and which come easily to us; the challenge is to show the same level of energy and initiative in subjects that are difficult, for which we don't have an affinity. Recommendations in this vein stand out because they are often extremely compelling.

To assist in your child's determination of which teachers to ask for recommendations, encourage him to consider these two main questions:

Question 1. Which teachers know me the best?

There are always going to be teachers with whom your child has a stronger relationship than others. Think within and beyond the classroom to answer this question. Any possible context outside the classroom experience can add a valuable, different perspective to the recommendation letter. Examples might include:

- athletic coach,
- activity adviser,
- theater or music group director,
- leader of a volunteer effort,
- someone who shares a common interest or talent.

Question 2. Which teachers like me the best?

This is a time for your child really to be honest and to assess what teachers might say about his performance, character, strengths, and weaknesses. One way to think about this is to look at some of the questions that most teachers are asked to provide in their recommendation letters, and ask your child to look at the questions from the teacher's perspective—to pretend to be in each teacher's shoes. To find these questions, I recommend looking at the Teacher Recommendation Form in the Common Application, which you can download from www.commonapp.org.

For each teacher under consideration, ask your child to write down how he thinks each teacher would respond to the following questions from the Common Application:

- What are the first words that come to your mind to describe this student?
- Please write whatever you think is important about this student, including a description of academic and personal characteristics. We are particularly interested in the candidate's intellectual

promise, motivation, maturity, integrity, independence, origi-
nality, initiative, leadership potential, capacity for growth, special talents, enthusiasm, concern for others, respect accorded by
faculty, and reaction to setbacks. We welcome information that
will help us to differentiate this student from others.

- Teachers are asked to rate the student on the following characteristics, compared to other college-bound students in his or
  her secondary school class, using these parameters: Below Average, Average, Good (above average), Very Good (well above average), Excellent (top 10 percent), Outstanding (top 5 percent),
  or One of the top few encountered in my career.

  - **creative, original thought;**
  - **motivation;**
  - **self-confidence;**
  - **independence, initiative;**
  - **intellectual ability;**
  - **academic achievement;**
  - **written expression of ideas;**
  - **effective class discussion;**
  - **disciplined work habits;**
  - **potential for growth.**

Once your child has made an honest assessment of which teachers
know and like him best, there is one more factor to consider: Do
these teachers have good anecdotes, stories, and examples about
your child? As with the college essays, the best recommendations
are ones that show, rather than tell. It's a safe bet to say that the
strongest recommendations, the ones that stand out amidst all the
others, are the ones with concrete examples.

WARNING! CHOOSE WISELY

Remind your child that this is a time for honest appraisal.
Usually, recommendations are confidential, meaning the student does not read the recommendation. Either the teacher

or guidance counselor mails the recommendation directly to the college or university. (Some teachers do give the student a copy of the recommendation, as a courtesy.) Given the blind nature of this process, students need to be absolutely sure that they will be receiving strong recommendations.

If teachers feel they would write a negative letter for a student, they will almost always decline the request. It is more problematic, therefore, to ask a teacher who will write a so-so recommendation. A so-so recommendation is a sign to an admissions officer that a student either asked the wrong teacher or didn't have a close enough relationship with any teacher to secure a better recommendation.

The bottom line: if your child has any doubts that a recommendation will be positive, he should ask a different teacher.

DON'T PANIC! WHAT IF MY CHILD HAS RESERVATIONS ABOUT ALL OF HIS TEACHERS?

Sometimes it happens that a student does not feel that any teachers know or like him particularly well. One hopes this is not the case, but if your child feels uncomfortable asking any teacher for recommendations, here are a few suggestions:

- Encourage your child to meet with some teachers to see if his feelings are real, or if his fears are imaginary. Making the effort to set up meetings will also increase the likelihood that these teachers would write something positive.
- Ask your child to choose the "lesser of all evils." Since recommendations are required by most schools, he has to choose someone, so discuss who would have the most positive things to say, even if the person is not ideal.

Step 3. Ask (early!)

Once your child has decided which two teachers to ask for recommendations, the key is to ask *early*. Typically, most students wait until fall of senior year. But, if possible, the best time to approach teachers is in late spring of junior year, before final exams hit and definitely before students and teachers leave for summer vacation.

Why so early? Obviously, to beat the rush. Fall of senior year is an incredibly busy time for teachers as well as students. Since the majority of students wait to ask in the fall, by asking in the spring your child will impress teachers with his foresight and initiative—traits that hopefully they will remember when writing about your child. More important, your child is giving them the courtesy of time—the entire summer to write the recommendation, when they have more opportunity to focus on your child and are not overwhelmed with work. The end result will be a much more thoughtfully prepared and well-written recommendation—and a much more appreciative teacher, I assure you.

NEW RULE OF COLLEGE ADMISSIONS: TEACHER MOVEMENT

Keep in mind that there is more unpredictability in the job market today. Teachers don't always return to the same job or school in the fall, for a variety of reasons. Some teachers retire, take maternity leave, or switch schools and/or careers. Most of these decisions about whether or not to return are made before the end of the school year. Even if a teacher is not returning the next year, it's still perfectly fine to submit the recommendation and asking for a recommendation early allows your child to get contact information and saves the inevitable scrambling to track down a former teacher in the fall.

Similarly, if your child has attended more than one high school, it is perfectly fine to ask a teacher from a former school. Working with an additional high school to secure the letter may prove a bit more logistically challenging, but can certainly be done if your child has a good relationship with the teacher. What is most important is getting a recommendation from a teacher who knows your child the best.

Some students don't want to approach teachers earlier, in the spring of junior year, because they don't yet have a final list of schools they want to attend. This shouldn't be a concern; teachers can still write a recommendation letter over the summer. Then in the fall, once the student's application list is finalized and he has the applications from each school, he should follow up with teachers. He can then provide them with the necessary forms—Common Application, or otherwise—and appropriate envelopes.

How should your child actually make the big request? He should ask in person, one-on-one with the teacher, either after class or at any other time when he can have the teacher's full attention. Your child should explain why he is asking the teacher for a recommendation and mention, if possible, some of the schools to which he is applying and the criteria for selecting particular colleges on his list. The conversation can go something like this:

"Hi, Mrs. Smith. As you know, I'm going to be applying to colleges next fall, and I know that my teacher recommendations are a very important piece of my college applications. I've enjoyed your class, and I would greatly appreciate if you would write a recommendation for me. Would you be willing to write a letter that discusses your impressions of my strengths, talents, and achievements?"

At College Coach we always recommend that students ask teachers in person, rather than by letter or e-mail; it is simply more personal and thoughtful. We also highly discourage parents from becoming involved in the request. This is the job of the child alone.

WARNING! A "YES" IS NOT GUARANTEED

Do not assume that teachers will always say yes to the request to write a recommendation for your child. Be sure to discuss with your student that a "no" is a possibility. Teachers, particularly in larger public schools, may set limits on the number of students for whom they will write recommendations. This is all the more reason to ask as early as possible.

In some instances, teachers may decline to write a letter because they don't feel they can write something positive. This "no" ultimately helps your child, because it is better for a teacher to turn down your child's request than to write a negative letter. Above all, you want your child to have the most positive recommendations possible.

Step 4. Make the recommender's job easy

The next step is for your child to give the teachers some assistance in putting together the best and most thorough recommendations possible—recommendations that are both effective and in sync with your child's all-important application theme. The best way to do this is by writing a "personal data letter" that goes into depth about your child's goals, involvements, future plans, or anything else he feels is pertinent for the teacher. The letter should contain:

- information about the student's goals and what he is looking to achieve in college;
- accomplishments of which he is most proud;
- elements that he will be highlighting in his portion of the application, specifically the application theme;
- a sample activities chart;
- a list of nonschool-related activities, volunteer work, work experience, or other commitments.

Even though this may seem like too much information, it provides the teachers with a greater perspective, a context within which they can write. It also serves to jog the teacher's memory. For example, the teacher may look at the student's chart and remember attending a performance or athletic event in which the student played a key role. The teacher may be able to refer to an article in the school newspaper that the student wrote that was particularly impressive. All in all, providing this information gives teachers tools they can use to create a much more comprehensive and in-depth recommendation, one that ultimately will allow an admissions committee to get a much more complete picture of the student.

PARENT TO-DO: PERSONAL DATA LETTER TEMPLATE

You can help your child prepare the personal data letter. It is important this letter provides the writer with good background information, so the actual writing process will go smoothly and be complete and thorough. *(Customize this template to suit your needs.)*

Dear _____,

    Thank you for agreeing to write a recommendation that will increase my chances of getting into the right school. I am writing this letter so that you can learn a little more about me. I hope this information is useful as you write your letter.

    I really enjoyed the class I took with you. I learned a lot from

_____.

    When I get to college, I plan to study _____ because _____.

    After college, I might _____.

    In addition to academics, I have been involved in _____.

    I am applying to these schools: _____.

    I am interested in these schools because _____.

    I have put a lot of thought into how I want schools to see me. Through my essays and extracurricular activities, I'm going to show that I _____.

    Thank you for agreeing to write a recommendation that will assist me in the application process. I'll keep you posted.

Sincerely,

Student

    Your child should also provide recommenders with a list of the schools he is applying to attend, and if possible, his intended major. Some teachers may choose to customize their letters to specific colleges. For instance, if the teacher is a graduate of the school, that can be a plus, as admissions officers might feel that teacher knows more about what would be a good fit for the school.

Step 5. Help your child manage deadlines

As soon as your child has his recommenders and has a final list of schools (usually fall of senior year), he should provide the recommending teachers with *all* of the appropriate forms (either the Common Application teacher recommendation form or an individual school's own form) for each school, as well as addressed and stamped envelopes for each school on the list. Your child should also provide teachers with the deadlines for each school, especially if he is applying early decision or early action to a particular school.

Colleges expect students to submit their portion of the application on time, but they understand that recommendations, transcripts, and test scores come in separately, and often after the deadline. That said, at College Coach we usually recommend that a student give teachers a deadline that is about a week prior to the college's application deadline. This way, the student can be sure that the recommendation gets in the mail at the appropriate time, so the application gets processed and read sooner rather than later.

Bear in mind that individual colleges have different requirements and preferences as to how the recommendations should be sent. Some prefer, or even require, that they receive the entire application, including the transcript and the recommendations, in one envelope. This saves some larger schools the monstrous task of opening and filing hundreds of thousands of individual recommendations. It is important to make sure your child knows the specific requirements for each school on his list and instructs recommendation writers accordingly.

A couple of weeks before the deadline, make sure that your child follows up with teachers. A brief conversation will suffice, or an e-mail message is fine and appropriate. They may not need the reminder, but just in case, it's a good practice to adopt. Here is some recommended language:

"Hi, Mrs. Smith. Thanks again for agreeing to write a letter of recommendation for my college applications. As the deadlines approach, I am working on my college applications. Just checking in with you to make sure you have everything you need. Thank you!"

Also, your child will want to check in with the college admissions office as well, to make sure they have received everything. Give the admissions offices a few weeks after the deadline, however, to allow them the time to open, sort, and file the admissions materials and credentials they've received. Many schools now allow students to track their application status online, especially if they've applied online, so that may be a better option.

III. ADDITIONAL LETTERS OF RECOMMENDATION

Other than the teacher recommendations that are required by colleges, you may find there are other people in the student's life that could provide an admissions committee a different and unique perspective. Probably the most frequent question I am asked about recommendations is regarding the submission of supplemental recommendations from people other than teachers. Should the student submit them, even though they're not required? And if so, how many? From whom?

While not required, an additional recommendation from someone who has worked with the student outside of the classroom setting can highlight another aspect. Some examples of this would be a letter from a coach, theater director, newspaper/yearbook adviser, a youth group adviser, or even an employer. But don't go overboard. Sending an additional one (two at most) is fine, but any more and a different message is sent to the admissions committee. Bear in mind that admissions officers have thousands, in many cases tens of thousands, of applications to read. Too many recommendations will overwhelm and even annoy an admissions reader and may cause that reader to question why so much information is included. It may signal a red flag of over-compensation on the part of the student, or even desperation. My advice is to choose carefully and make sure that an additional recommendation will add something significant and valuable to your child's application.

Students should also avoid sending recommendations from peers or family members, unless specifically requested by the college. Some schools, such as Dartmouth College, do invite an optional "peer recommendation," which can be from a peer or family member, such as a cousin or close aunt. Other schools invite parents to write a letter, so that they can provide their own unique perspectives (Brandeis does this, among several other institutions). If a college or university invites it, feel free, but *only* if they invite it. In that case, be sure your child chooses carefully. The writer should be someone who has seen your child in a "role" that he or she can discuss in detail, such as in a music group, on a sports team, or in a work environment. If possible, this letter should work in your child's application theme as well.

WARNING! THICK FOLDERS DO NOT NECESSARILY IMPRESS

I strongly urge you to avoid recommendations from alumni, board members, or big donors to the college if they don't' know your child personally. The "friend of a friend of my second cousin's roommate who is on the alumni board at Brown" probably isn't going to make any difference in your child's application—unless your child has worked for her or has had some other significant interaction. And a student should never send a generic recommendation from a congressman or state senator unless the politician actually knows the student well. Even if the student interned in the politician's office—if he did not work closely with the person, don't bother with a recommendation. This type of ploy can hurt your child more than help him.

IV. REMEMBER TO SAY THANK YOU

There is one last task to do before all is said and done: your child should be sure to formally thank his teachers, guidance counselor, and any others who wrote recommendation letters promptly after the recommendation is sent. Don't allow your child to wait until the colleges send their decisions—that won't be for several months. It is good etiquette and simply the right thing to do, to thank people for their efforts. Your child should express his appreciation for the time and effort they put into writing the recommendations. Never just assume that it's "part of their job" for teachers or counselors. It takes a vast amount of work and time to write good recommendations, on top of all of their other huge responsibilities. They should be thanked accordingly.

Letters of recommendation are not prepared by your child, but they can be managed to help provide as much benefit as possible. Remind your child to start early, be prepared, ask strategically, and graciously thank all recommenders, and he can make the most of this portion of the application.

CHAPTER 9

INTERVIEWS

Expert Coach: Lloyd Peterson,
Vice President of Education, College Coach, and
Former Senior Admissions Officer, Yale University

Interviews can be nerve-wracking for teenagers. It took me a while to realize this as an admissions officer, but most students wish they didn't have to interview at all. The notion of sharing personal ambitions and passions with a complete stranger is daunting, even for adults. Additionally, the interview is associated with a lot of uncertainty: Whom will I meet with? What will she ask? What is the right thing to say? However frightening it may be, the interview is a unique opportunity for your child to stand out in the admissions process. It is one of the few chances a student has to personalize his candidacy.

For this important reason, the on-campus and/or alumni interview should be a cornerstone of your college planning strategy, even though it is not typically required. In the interview, the admissions officer is seeking information not found on the transcript or inferred from standardized testing: information about friends, family, likes, dislikes, free time, books read, and movies seen, what makes a child happy and sad. These are the personal attributes that help admissions decide if your child is a good match for the institution. Ultimately, this information is shared with the admissions committee to help shed light on a given student and affect the ultimate yes or no decision.

If your child knows what to expect from the interview process and prepares effectively, he can make the most of this important and exciting opportunity.

RULES TO REMEMBER IN THIS CHAPTER

- **Interview situations vary.** College interviewers come in many forms: senior or junior admissions office staff members, alumni representatives, and student ambassadors. They all count. By recognizing the likely scenario that accompanies each type of interviewer, your child can feel more confident and comfortable by knowing what is expected and likely to happen.
- **Presentation matters.** The interview is as much about what the student says as how he says it. Students must be appropriately dressed, well-mannered, and poised.
- **Remind your child to answer the "Why?"** Interview questions are designed to highlight a student's personality, values, and beliefs. Interviewers want to know what the student would be like as a member of the college community. Encourage your child to prepare for college interviews by thinking about his curiosity behind certain interests and his passion for certain activities. Detailed, creative answers are the best answers.
- **The interview doesn't end with the final handshake.** Thank-you notes are the essential last step of an interview. Don't let your child forget this final point of etiquette.

NEW RULE OF COLLEGE ADMISSIONS: INTERVIEWS MATTER MORE

How much of a difference can an interview make? Admit, wait list, defer, and reject are the decisions made regarding an applicant. Over the years, I have rarely seen an interview move an applicant up two positions on this continuum, say from reject to admit. In fairness, though, neither can a prolific arm that could throw a football fifty yards or gifted fingers that played virtuoso-concert level piano. A strong interview can move an applicant one step up the ladder, from reject to wait list, or even better—wait list to admit.

Make sure your student is aware of the significance a strong interview can have on admissions success.

I. TYPES OF INTERVIEWS

Colleges differ in their interview methods, so check with the schools on your child's list to see what they offer. Here is an overview of the most common types of interviews you are likely to encounter.

On-Campus Interviews

The summer between junior and senior year is often considered interview season, and August is the busiest interview month. Tours and information sessions during August are jam-packed with prospective applicants. Another popular interview week is during spring break of junior year. So, if you and your child plan to visit campuses during spring vacation, make sure to schedule your interview well in advance. A month beforehand is optimal; two weeks in advance should be the minimum lead time.

During interview season, most colleges offer prospective applicants either an "informational" (nonevaluative) or an "evaluative" interview. The only difference between the two is that an evaluative interview always results in a report from the interviewer and an informational interview may not. Be aware, however, that informational interviews are also evaluative, and your child should prepare for and attend any type of interview a college offers, no matter which "type" it is. Why the different types? Ideally, every college would interview every applicant, but most do not have the staff to do this, so they offer optional informational interviews. One advantage of this system for the colleges is that this optional interview helps them determine which students are most interested in attending their school. While schools that offer informational interviews say that these interviews are not required, I always recommend signing up and having your child take them just as seriously as evaluative interviews.

The interviews do not differ much in format. Both are good, old-fashioned one-on-one conversations. Your child should provide an oral snapshot of who he is, what his academic interests are, and what extracurricular activities he enjoys. Admissions officers, in turn, will probe to see if your child and the college are a good fit, academically and personally. Your child has the chance to ask questions and have questions answered. The only difference, again, is that a report is written at the end of an evaluative interview. The report is filed with the application and reviewed with other admissions materials before a decision is made.

Follow the procedures of the schools on your child's list to determine what type of interview they require.

WARNING! INFORMATIONAL INTERVIEWS COUNT

Despite what the name might say, informational interviews might prove to be just as evaluative as officially "evaluative" interviews. Your child should follow all of the same guidelines to prepare for an informational interview as he would for an evaluative interview. Informational interviews can—and often do—result in write-ups just like evaluative interviews. Schools would not offer these interviews if they did not count for something. An admissions officer who meets a student at an informational interview will likely voice an opinion about the student when the student's application is eventually assessed.

There are other interview variations as well. Sometimes information interviews are conducted with a small group of students. For thirty to forty-five minutes, students, usually as bright and as curious as yours, benefit from each other's questions and answers.

Moreover, telephone interviews are not unusual when colleges are recruiting students who live abroad. Make sure your child is aware that every interview matters and he should be prepared and polite for any interaction related to the colleges he wants to attend.

Alumni Interviews

Some colleges and universities that interview on campus also offer alumni interviews. These are held in your local community, often at the alum's place of employment, or even in the interviewer's home or in a mutually convenient coffee shop. Follow each college's procedure as to whether your child should schedule an alumni interview.

Alumni interviewers volunteer their time to interview, and therefore have great enthusiasm for their alma maters. Despite the passion displayed by a volunteer interviewer from the Class of 1965, admission offices understand that today's college environments are different. Subsequently, all individuals are screened, and participation in ongoing training and campus updates is mandatory.

As an admissions officer conducting interviews, I tried my best to be cordial, fair, and entertaining, but always impartial. I wore a pretty good poker face during my interviews. Admissions officers like working with adolescents, but the best interviewers are informative and supportive, yet never leading. No winking, no nodding once the interview is over. Alumni, on the other hand, have a different role. Alumni admissions representatives serve as institutional ambassadors in their local communities. In part, their job is to raise the college's visibility in the community by attending the local college fair, interviewing students for admission, and so on. Ideally, their job also is to increase admissions activity from that area, which means improving (or sustaining) the number of applicants, admits, and enrollees. No one is fired if the numbers don't improve, but alumni who volunteer for such work take it very seriously.

Alumni interviewers want your child to do well. In this case, poker faces are left at the poker table. Friendly behavior is typical when your teen arrives at their door. Enthusiasm, however, will never supersede loyalty. Despite intended goodwill and neighborly relations, alum interviewers care deeply about their schools and take their jobs very seriously. If, in their eyes, your child cannot hold his own, especially from a social or maturational view, loyalty to school usually wins.

WARNING! DON'T LET YOUR CHILD "BLOW OFF" AN ALUMNI INTERVIEW

Even though alumni interviews may be more casual than on-campus interviews with admissions officers, they still count and can help or hurt your child's chances. Your child should not take the alumni interview any less seriously than an on-campus interview. Be sure that your teen follows all of the advice in this chapter whether he is interviewing with an admissions officer or an alum.

Student Interviews

In addition to on-campus and alumni interviews, some colleges hire and train students to interview. These are college juniors and seniors who have normally worked for the admissions office in another capacity, such as hosting overnight guests or giving tours. They know the ins and outs of the college.

Admissions offices use students for a couple of reasons. Some colleges need the extra people power, most often during the fall, when most officers are away recruiting. Other offices think it makes good sense to provide applicants with a college student viewpoint. Admissions officers get older each year, but the cohort with whom they work remains eighteen to twenty-one years old.

The use of college students to interview concerns some parents and prospective applicants, but it shouldn't. These students have been carefully selected and thoroughly trained. And they do provide a perspective different than a two-decade veteran's. Student interviewers write evaluations and affect admissions decisions just like interview reports from admissions officers, so your child should be thoroughly prepared, polite, and polished if he attends an interview with a student. They "count" just the same.

II. PREPARING YOUR CHILD FOR INTERVIEWS

Preparation for the college interview is absolutely crucial. By discussing the information in this chapter with your child, you can be sure he is primed for interview success. Interviewers are not trying to trick students or trip them up; they simply want to get to know the students beyond their transcripts and written applications. Kids should treat interviews as opportunities to shine and show their personalities, rather than scary experiences where they are on the spot.

While all of the various interviews described in the previous section are important and require the same level of preparation, from this point on I will focus on the most common type: the on-campus interview conducted by an admissions officer.

Deciding When and Where to Interview

Interviews are almost never a requirement for admission to a school, but I think it is a bad decision not to interview at all. Admissions offices track interviews and use them as a measure of interest, so if your child wants to interview at a school, he should do his best to schedule an interview there. Ideally, if you have the time and money is not an issue, your child should interview at all of the schools on his list. However, since in many cases time and money are factors, students often need to prioritize. In this case, I recommend that your child interview with as many schools as possible, with an emphasis on the schools he most wants to attend.

However, since most students are nervous about interviewing, it's best for your child's very first interview experience to be at a school from his Just Right or No Problem list. This strategy alleviates some of the pressure, and related mistakes made in the first interview, or first few interviews.

Getting Ready

Rule 1. Dress to Impress

First impressions are important. Just as colleges spend energy and resources so that their school makes a good impression, so your child should strive to make a good first impression. First impressions are lasting impressions.

Armani suits and Saks Fifth Avenue dresses aren't necessary. In fact, the rules are few and simple:

Boys: Blazers are optional, but popular in certain geographic regions like the Northeast. The same applies for neckties. Shirts must have collars; slacks or khakis are preferred. Socks are a must, and sneakers are a no-no. Baseball caps or other hats are also forbidden.

Girls: Female candidates have more decisions to make: the dress versus the blouse-and-skirt outfit next to a pant-blouse, and perhaps, jacket combination! Frankly, any of these choices is fine. But jeans and sneakers are not appropriate for anyone, female or male. I get lots of questions regarding makeup for young women. If your daughter doesn't wear makeup regularly, then the college interview is not the place to experiment. And less is usually more appropriate.

Here is a list of additional dos and don'ts to share with your student:

- If your want to wear cologne or perfume, **do** cut the dose in half on interview day.
- Don't wear your sunglasses on top of your head or hanging from your collar. Put them away when you arrive.
- Do turn off cell phones, pagers, BlackBerries, portable video games, iPods and any other electronics; stow them in a bag or briefcase or leave them in the lobby.
- Don't wear scuffed shoes or wrinkled clothes. Make the effort to be neat and polished.
- Don't wear anything ripped, overly tight, or low-cut. What may be in fashion at school or at the mall is not necessarily appropriate for a college interview. When in doubt, err on the side of being more conservative and formal. Most parents can help their children judge what is acceptable.

Rule 2. Brush Up on Manners 101

Preparing your child for college interviews may also require a brush-up on manners. Even the best-dressed applicant can spoil an interview by rudeness or disrespect. It's nearly impossible to flunk an interview, to say something so inflammatory or egregious that, despite other charms, the student is not wanted on campus. However, it has happened. Students have a right to their own opinion, and the support of First Amendment rights are alive and well on college campuses. Still, it's a good rule of thumb and common sense to steer clear of certain subjects. Racist, sexist, and homophobic remarks are not acceptable; negative comments toward the elderly, and physically or mentally challenged reflect poor taste and bad judgment. Enough said.

While your child doesn't need to read through a Miss Manners book before each interview, he should keep in mind the following essentials of etiquette:

- Do refer to the interviewer as "Mr." or "Ms." unless otherwise instructed.
- Don't curse under any circumstances.
- Don't chew gum or suck on cough drops, mints, or other candy. Chewing gum is known to calm nerves, but it is impolite in an interview.
- Do sit up straight and sit with legs crossed or feet flat on the floor.
- Do express yourself in clear, mature language. Avoid colloquial phrases such as "like" and "you know."

If your child is not the most naturally eloquent of kids, the manners component of interviewing may take a little bit of honing. Practice with your child, or even tape him during a mock interview conversation to check for overuse of certain words or filler words such as "um" or "uh." Ultimately the goal is for your child to appear poised—confident, well-spoken, and gracious. If your child feels uncomfortable conducting a mock interview with you, enlist the help of a professional relative or family friend.

Perhaps the best advice to students about manners: don't do anything during an interview that you wouldn't do at a dinner party. Or in front of your grandmother.

Rule 3. Arrive Early

Your child should plan to get to the interview a few minutes early. If the interview is on campus, there may be forms to complete, so a ten- to fifteen-minute cushion is usually helpful. Ideally, your child can also use this extra time to relax and collect his thoughts before heading into the interview.

III. BEHIND CLOSED DOORS: INSIDE THE INTERVIEW

Will memorizing the names of the entire biology faculty or firing off a list of impressive graduates impress the interviewer? It's not necessary for your child to memorize anything. Looking inward is more important than reviewing Web sites and talking to others. To help your student thoroughly prepare, ask him to ponder questions that fall in two categories:

1. What do you have to offer the institution? What contributions will you make to the freshman community academically, athletically, artistically, scientifically, culturally?
2. What does the college have to offer you? Can the school meet your academic needs? Can it meet your personal (athletic, artistic, scientific, cultural) needs as well?

Unlike the college essay that can be corrected and revised before submitting, the interview is in "real time." You cannot unring a bell; once a comment is made, it's made. No proofs, no revisions. Preparation for the interview questions is therefore vital. To get them past the tough questions, have your child spend more time looking inward. The applicant should be the star of the interview show and in charge of the situation. This is critical for creating an impression that the student is ready to go to college and be responsible for himself.

    In this section I will analyze each stage of a typical interview and offer tips for your child to prepare for each portion. When I was training new admissions officers or recent graduates planning to volunteer as alumni interviewers, I divided the thirty-minute interview into thirds. This is the template I will use below.

But First . . . the Handshake

When the admissions officer arrives to greet your child in the lobby, that is the moment the interview begins. It may seem like an informal moment, but first impressions matter. Be sure your child stands to greet the admissions officer, smiles, and offers a polite handshake. This will get the interview started on the right foot.

Interviewing 101: The "Big Three" Opening Questions

In the first third of an interview, I always worked on the "Big Three." They are the three questions that inevitably emerge within the interview's first ten minutes, namely:

- Why are you applying here?
- What are your academic interests?
- What are your extracurricular activities?

These questions, in some version, find their way into interviews early on, because they are extremely relevant. They also are easy questions to ask and to answer. Let's look at each question in detail:

The question: Why are you applying here?

With nearly four thousand colleges in the United States, "Why are you applying to our college?" is an appropriate question. To help your child prepare to answer this question, you can revisit those earlier college list conversations to review your child's list drivers.

The best answer

The ideal answer to this question should explain how the college meets the students' academic needs and extracurricular needs.

For instance, Sarah might say that she wants to attend Connecticut College because she is impressed by its vibrant English department and also wants to take advantage of the sailing team. Answers should be creative and specific, and, as much as possible, relate to the student's application theme.

The question: What are your academic interests?

This question often leads to a discussion of what the student may choose as a major. Regarding a major, the "undecided box" on the college application is quite popular. If your teenager has no clue, don't worry. But when you are helping your child prepare, do probe him about his most favorite and least favorite subjects.

The best answer

This question is best answered by addressing your child's academic interest—to show passion for certain subjects. Also make sure your child knows where he stands on elective courses and foreign languages. Students have options when choosing both, and choices reflect interest and values—and impresses an admissions officer.

The question: What are your extracurricular interests?

I tended to address this issue by asking a student how he keeps busy on weekends and after school. I asked students to begin with grade nine, but encouraged them to go back further if they thought it was relevant and interesting. More important, I wanted to know why students liked particular activities. If a boy doesn't plan to play professional soccer, and has no plans to coach, why has he played the game, year after year, come rain or shine?

The best answer

To prepare for activities questions, don't ask your daughter to describe her favorite activity. Instead, ask her about her "curiosity" in that activity. What excites her about art? What originally made her become involved in sculpture? What is her favorite place to practice her art? Move beyond what your child does and peel back to the "why." When it comes to impressing an interviewer, it's not about the win-loss record in a sport or the number of violin concertos a student can play, rather it's about uncovering the passion behind an activity.

Interviewing 101: Open-Ended Questions

The transition from the first to the middle third of an interview is usually seamless. One minute, your child is humming along, talking about premed aspirations and his backhand. Then the questions change. For colleges that offer evaluative interviews, the middle of the conversation is fertile ground for deeper questions that evoke and provoke. The questions during the middle third are open-ended and encourage students to share their values and beliefs. Admissions officers seek to find what's important to your child: family, friends, religion, integrity, honesty, and so on. Again, this helps an admissions officer determine how your child would fit into the campus community.

Open-ended questions are also designed to highlight or illuminate certain personality traits. For example, I favored the question "Describe your most nervous moment last year." Your daughter answers: "I'm on my school's varsity hoops team. Mom and Dad were in the stands. The score is tied, with one second to go, and I'm at the free-throw line!"

Whether she made the shot isn't where I focus my attention. I'm concentrating on the humility displayed if the shot went in or the courage displayed if she missed it. The personality traits "tied to" the activity is what we seek. An interviewer cares less that an applicant was the team captain and more that the student can express what kind of experience it was to be a member of the team. If your child has not been a team captain, club president, or lead in the school play, he can still show his leadership skills, ability to be a team player, or other positive traits in the way he talks about his experiences in the interview.

NEW RULE OF COLLEGE ADMISSIONS: CHARACTER GETS NOTICED

When admissions officers are "presenting" a student to the rest of the admissions committee, they spend a great deal of time honing their messages regarding extracurricular activities. And titles—such as captain, president, and editor—are part of that message. However, in my experience, titles did not dominate committee discussions. Instead, these words and phrases did: ambition, resilience, curiosity, perseverance, humility, courage, maturity, creativity, leadership, and reaction to setback. The character traits tied to the activity find their way into interview reports and affect decisions just as much as impressive credentials. Of the thousands of reports I wrote, most of my prose came from the middle third of an interview when a student's personality came shining through.

How does your child prepare for the rigors of the open-ended middle third of the interview? Remember the two fundamental questions the admissions committee will ask about each applicant: Can this student do the work academically? And what will this student contribute socially, culturally, and personally, if we admit him to join our school community? As a parent, you can help your child prepare by asking related questions. Your child should write down his answers to organize his thoughts. Remind your child that there are no right or wrong answers. To move him forward in an interview, however, the follow-up question is more important. Again, the key question is "Why?" Why is soccer, the guitar, student council, or volunteer work important?

In your preparations, begin asking your child questions about ninth grade and work your way forward to the present. This is the tough part: pushing the rewind button, backing up three years, and reviewing it all. The good memories are fun, but your daughter cannot hide from that C+ in tenth-grade French. Nor can your son duck conversations that drift toward ninth-grade baseball, when he was cut from the team. So to fully practice for the interview, and the college process in general, students must review everything. They must pick out the strengths and passions, along with the wrinkles, and figure out how to talk about it in thirty minutes.

DON'T PANIC! WON'T TALKING ABOUT MISTAKES DRAW ATTENTION TO THE NEGATIVE?

Examples of mistakes, disappointments, or challenges may be addressed by your child during an interview. This is fine, and can in fact be a great opportunity for your child to impress an admissions officer with his ability to see seeming mistakes more as "learning opportunities." Events such as not making the varsity swim team, having one's voice crack during a choir solo, or losing the state debate championship can all be discussed for their positive impact on a child's growth. Interviewers are by no means looking for "perfect" students, and disappointments often reveal a student's depth of character.

Remind your child, however, that discussing mistakes or challenges does not mean making excuses. The interview is not the time to explain away a poor grade or record of multiple tardies.

Here are some specific questions to guide your child's preparation to answer academic open-ended questions.

- What courses have you taken that you truly enjoyed, and why?
- What courses might you take in college, even if they are not related to your potential major, and why?
- Since grade nine, which subjects were your most and least favorite?
- What are the similarities and differences *between* those subjects?

Regarding the last question, if your son enjoyed math and English, don't force him to choose a favorite. Instead, push him to find a common denominator between the two. Regardless of the subject, a connection always exists, and this can be another opportunity to emphasize the student's application theme—of leadership, community spirit, communications, public service, scientific inquiry, and so on.

Life outside the classroom should be subjected to the same self-interrogation.

- How have you spent your summers, and why?
- What activities are most important to you, and why?
- What extracurriculars have you enjoyed most and least, and why?

When reviewing extracurricular activities, it is important that non-school-based activities are included as well. Ballet, martial arts, and Scouting are important activities for youth in our society and are worth mentioning in the interview. In admissions circles, these activities carry as much weight as school-based sports, student government, and the arts.

PARENT TO-DO: REVIEW SAMPLE OPEN-ENDED QUESTIONS WITH YOUR CHILD

Through my years in admissions, and over the course of thousands of mock interviews, a "favorite questions" list evolved. In addition to the questions already provided in the text of this chapter, these trigger the most insightful answers, reveal a true sense of the student's personality, and are actually pretty fun, too. Try going over these questions with your child. Encourage him to open up and give real answers like he would provide during the actual interview.

Common interview questions
- What are some of your criteria for choosing a college?
- What do you plan to contribute?
- How would you describe your school?
- If you could change one thing about your high school, what would it be? Walk me through a typical day at school.
- Have you worked up to your potential in high school?

- What has been your biggest achievement?
- What's the most difficult situation you've faced?
- What do you want to do after you graduate from college?
- Have you ever thought of not going to college?
- What would you like to talk about?

MY PERSONAL FAVORITE INTERVIEW QUESTIONS

- What are your most favorite subjects since ninth grade? Least favorite subjects, and why?
- What is your most favorite activity, and why? Which activity takes up most of your time?
- Push the rewind button. You have just finished eighth and are about to enter ninth grade. You have the option to attend your current school. Or you can attend any high school in the nation. Would you attend your school or choose another?
- What kind of year did the school community have while you were in grade eleven? Not you personally, but the community—the teachers, administrators, and students? Was it business as usual? Or did something happen that surprised you, made you happy or angry?
- Describe or define your best friends. Are they much like you or are they very different? Talk about the similarities and differences.
- Describe what a "perfect day" would be for you.
- You've written an autobiography with nothing left to do but entitle it. What is the title of your autobiography?
- If you could play any instrument to perfection, which would it be?
- Switch places with your favorite teacher. Would you give yourself the same grade?
- What is your favorite book? How about your favorite movie? Discuss for me the commonalities between the two.

Granted, these are not the exact questions your child will receive during his interview, but they will likely be similar. Hopefully, this will give you and your child an idea of what to expect and help you to better prepare.

Interviewing 101: Final Impressions

With approximately ten minutes to go in an interview, I always wanted to shift gears again. At this point, your teen has made it through the middle third of open-ended questions and is coming down the home stretch. The student can sense it. The interviewer will likely ask a few of the more creative questions listed above or will ask the student to expand on an intriguing comment from earlier in the conversation. The interviewer is now trying to draw conclusions and solidify his opinion of the applicant: Do I like this kid? Will she fit? Will he add something? Is he the kind of guy we want here?

Before it's over, the interviewer will, for a couple of minutes at most, eloquently relate the college's virtues. This is not a sales pitch. I wasn't necessarily plugging my school; tours and information sessions do that. Instead, I always felt a need to place the interview in the larger context of the college. After my brief soliloquy, I always asked the student if he had any questions. This is the final stage of the interview.

Interviewing 101: Questions Students Can Ask the Interviewer

Some students get nervous during this final portion of the interview. One school of thought states that students must have a couple of solid questions to ask the interviewer. I, however, feel differently. I do not think your child needs good questions for the interviewer. But he does need to have a good response. If your child has a question, he should certainly ask it—and the best applicants generally have a question in mind, perhaps about a specific activity or class they have read about. If not, students should not waste the interviewer's time. Asking no question is better than asking a dumb one.

If a student doesn't have a question, a thoughtful response might be: "This school has been high on my list for some time so I've done a fair amount of research. The tour was also helpful, and this interview has given me a couple of new things to think about, but right now I don't have any questions. If something comes up, though, do you have a card or e-mail address where I can reach you?"

This answer is good because it has three components: In the first component, the interviewee takes ownership for his/her candidacy, "This school has been high on my list . . . I've done research. . . ." The interviewer is clear that the student is taking the application process and the interview very seriously. "I am a serious candidate for admission" is the message your son or daughter sends in the first component.

Stroking the interviewer, the second component, is savvy advice at age seventeen or at age twenty-seven. It just makes good sense. Teenagers often see this as brownnosing. Not so. There was nothing mushy about the example. It reflects savvy thinking and simply acknowledges a good conversation is winding down. And the third component, getting the business card, leaves the door open for further communication.

WARNING! TABOO QUESTIONS

Are there questions your child should not ask? Absolutely. Admissions-related questions are a no-no. "What kind of grade point average are you looking for?" or "Is there a cutoff for SATs?" and similar questions should never be asked. Your teen should know those answers before setting foot on campus. In addition, the question sends up red flags. If a student is competitive, why would he need to ask that question? Or, if a student is concerned with these answers, how competitive is he really? Those are thoughts you don't want running through an admissions officer's head.

Will interviewers stay away from admissions-related questions? Most do, but it varies. There is no visible pattern among schools that ask and those that don't, nor is there an obvious pattern between admissions officers versus alumni interviewers. Personally, I am against asking admissions-related questions in interviews. Your son or daughter may get a rookie, though. Then what happens? The question will come either directly or indirectly. "What is your grade point average and SAT composite?" is direct. An indirect question may sound like this, "Do you have any admissions-related questions I may answer?"

If an interviewer does ask a direct question, students must answer. When doing so, he should give the grade point average and SAT/ACT composite only (without breaking up into subscores). Then the student should sit quietly, with no editorializing. For instance, a child should not say: "My grade point average is a B+; it should be an A-, but my history teacher . . ." The student should simply sit, forcing the interviewer to move on. It is a bad question to ask in an interview, but it still may happen.

Be wary of the art portfolio, too. I believe visual arts have a place on college campuses, but I don't think the interview is the place to showcase your teen's talent. Thirty minutes of conversation is a more efficient use of the time. If your child does feel it's essential to bring an art portfolio or other visual, then the goal should be to talk about why he is interested in art and how he plans to pursue art at the college. The admissions officer is most likely not a good judge of the quality of the artwork anyway. Some interviewers may disagree, but most would prefer discussion with a student rather than a review of a portfolio.

Wrapping Up

Some interviewers try to end the conversation with a thought-provoking question instead of, "Thanks for coming and good luck!" Here's my question: "Press the fast-forward button. You graduated last night; the ink on your diploma is still wet. You awaken the next morning and at the foot of your bed you find an obscenely large pile of money. The money is yours, all of it, under one condition: you cannot go to college for two years. What would you do with that time, and all that money?"

I've asked the question for nearly two decades. For the longest time, kids had only one year. In the late '90s, I added a second year to the question, to make it a tougher decision. I like the question because the interview ends with an exchange about something your teen values.

Finally, remind your child that a handshake is customary after the interview. At the end of the interview, your teen's extending his hand should be as natural as standing. He shouldn't bother waiting on the interviewer; just stand and extend! Before leaving the admissions office, make certain your teen gets the interviewer's business card, or has the person's e-mail address and phone number written somewhere. If not, he can stop by the receptionist's desk to request this information, which is crucial for the final stage of the interview: the follow-up thank-you note.

Interview Follow-up

Interview follow-up includes a thank-you note to the interviewer, usually within a few days. Remind your child that the thank-you note need not be an essay. It's simply a polite note. In it, have your child thank the interviewer for his time, insight, and answers. Those are the basics. Anything else, such as personal anecdotes that sharpened a story's focus, or enriched a point, is above what's required. That, too, should be recognized. If an application is forthcoming, your child should mention that as well. If the application is already there and your teen would attend if admitted, by all means have your child write that! Years ago, such notes were crafted on fancy stationery, the envelope lined, the stamp perfectly placed. (I enjoyed those days!) Today, e-mail is welcomed, equally effective, and more efficient.

IV. HOW THE INTERVIEW IS EVALUATED

Now that your child's work is done, let's look at how the interview is reported by the interviewer. The interviewer's final evaluation is critical for other committee members to make an informed decision regarding admission. Note that an on-campus interviewer may or may not be the person who initially reads your child's application, so the written evaluation of the interview is a very important document.

The End Report

After the interview concludes, and you and your hopeful child leave for the campus tour, the interviewer will sit down to write a summary. The interviewer will ask himself: How did the interview go? What did I learn about this student? What impressions did I receive? Then he will write up a report. The report helps all the other admissions officers to get a better sense of the student as a whole. Hopefully, it will provide enough insight to make the final admissions decision more cut-and-dry.

SAMPLE EVALUATIVE INTERVIEW REPORT

Jeremy's thirty minutes flew by; he is a very engaging kid. He jumped all over the "why us" question, speaking knowledgeably about the volunteer opportunities and intramural athletic facilities. Plus, he spoke highly of the city, and on a rainy day no one speaks highly of this city. He gets a point.

Big theater résumé, from community playhouses to regional theaters. He acts but wants to direct. He brought a "director's packet" for a proposed play. Looks like a lot of work, and he is fully immersed. Impressive. Also has sports and student council, with some leadership. He pushes the envelope a bit; not rowdy, but not afraid to take a stand. He's clearly visible around school.

His stock began to rise when describing his "posse," as he put it. He's a self-proclaimed "redheaded, left-handed, half-Jewish, half-Catholic, football playing, theater director." I liked the depth of answers as he reflected on a recent anti-Semitic mishap at school. He stood behind his beliefs when everyone else seemed to freeze. They followed him, and the school acknowledged.

We moved on. I asked about his visibility and he downplayed it. Three years earlier he was eighty-five pounds heavier and quite unpopular. Loses the weight, makes the team, gets the girl, blah, blah, blah . . .

But what I liked was the manner in which he dissects the difference between being popular and being well liked. "I don't have a lot of friends, but we respect each other. If kids at school get behind me on principle, well that's cool too. But it's just who I am. I think that's well-respected." He goes on, "I know people who aren't laughing with some of the really popular kids. They are laughing *at* 'em."

Down to earth, balanced, and self-assured, Jeremy did a wonderful job, and he gained nice steam along the way, finishing strong. I like this kid's spunk. If his numbers hold I'm inclined to lean green. *(Translated: if grades and testing are competitive, I will probably vote to admit.)*

PARENT TO-DO: INTERVIEW CHECKLIST

Although it seems like a lot of information to retain, visiting a campus and participating in an interview can easily be a manageable task. However, there are many things for you and your child to keep track of regarding interviews. Following is a checklist you can use to help ensure your child is on the right track to completing a successful interview. This should tie up any loose ends and take away some of the stress, so your child can arrive focused and ready.

Interview Checklist

Before leaving

____ Call well in advance to schedule appointment

____ Get directions, address, phone number

____ Organize notes on campus and surrounding community

____ Agree on attire

While en route, review—once more
___Academic/intellectual interests
___Personal beliefs and values
___Extracurricular passions

Once there
___Arrive early at admissions office; check in
___Learn interviewer's name
___Stop by the bathroom, glance in the mirror.
___Gather yourself. Take slow, deep breaths. Don't worry. You're ready.

Afterward
___Process the interview with friends and family right away
___Make note of areas that went well and those that need work
___Send a thoughtful thank-you note
___Inform college counselor

In the end, remember that a good interview involves a teen who is excited to learn how a college can meet his academic and personal needs. He answers questions analytically, not just descriptively. He will make certain the interviewer knows what his greatest contribution will be. And that no matter how small, it will be hugely significant. He also will soak up the information provided, leaving with every hope that it is not the best college, but rather the right college.

The interviewer, in turn, will be enthusiastic about the college he represents and about engaging each applicant for thirty minutes. An expert on the college and on the admissions process, the interviewer is looking for a good match, a good roommate, and someone who will contribute to the community. When all is said and done, after all the tips and insights, what truly makes an effective college interview? Great college interviews are great conversations.

CHAPTER 10

PAYING FOR COLLEGE

Expert Coach: Robert Weinerman, Former Manager, Financial Aid Delivery, Massachusetts Institute of Technology

Many families find the financial aid process challenging. There are many forms to fill out, questions to answer, requests from colleges to remember. Nonetheless, it's well worth the effort; billions of dollars of financial aid are distributed to millions of students every year.

Just as the admissions process is strategic and deadline driven, so too is the financial aid process. This chapter will fully explain the philosophies behind financial aid, explain the complexities of the financial aid application process, and recommend ways to secure additional scholarship money from colleges and other organizations. With strategy, early planning, and timely submission of all required forms, many families have the opportunity to benefit from various types of financial assistance to offset the significant cost of college.

RULES TO REMEMBER IN THIS CHAPTER

- **Understand the system.** The federal and state governments, colleges, and other scholarship providers play a critical role in determining what type and how much aid will be provided to a family. Knowing who "controls" what is the first step to maximizing the ultimate financial award you may receive.

- **Get a head start on the competition.** Start a scholarship search early both to increase the chances that a student will be a good candidate for scholarship money and to simplify and streamline the scholarship application process. Additionally, integrating financial considerations into the college selection and application process enhances a student's chances of winning scholarships from the colleges themselves.

- **Be strategic.** Applying to colleges at which the student is an exceptional or unusual candidate creates opportunities for colleges to use scholarships to recruit the student. And applying to colleges that are rivals in the admissions process enhances the likelihood of success in negotiation for additional financial aid.

- **Share unusual circumstances.** Financial aid formulas may not capture your family's full financial picture, and colleges want to understand any unusual circumstances that affect your family's ability to afford their institution. You can maximize your financial aid award by explaining unusual circumstances, either through a thoughtful letter prior to the release of your financial aid award or in a formal appeal subsequent to receiving your award.

I. HOW FINANCIAL AID WORKS

Every college makes its own, independent decisions for both admissions and financial aid. They determine which applicants to invite to join their next class, and they decide how much and what type of financial aid a student is eligible to receive. However, one place the admissions and financial aid processes differ is the extent to which the college's authority extends. While the admissions decision applies exclusively to the education offered by the college, the financial aid decisions that the college makes apply not only to college funds, but also to federal and state government funds. Colleges administer federal, state, and college funds based on rules established by the Department of Education, Congress, the State Higher Education Authorities, and the college it-self, respectively.

This means that even though a student submits an application for federal aid to the Department of Education, the college determines the student's eligibility for federal aid. Most states leave the determination of state aid to the individual colleges as well. The Department of Education simply processes the application data that the student provides, ensuring that the application is complete, and sends it to the colleges for interpretation.

The college also works with the student to ensure that the student meets all the requirements to receive the government funds, such as signing promissory notes, meeting satisfactory academic progress requirements, and achieving appropriate levels of academic credit. Finally, after the student has met the requirements for federal and state financial aid, the college—not the student—receives the funds on the student's behalf.

When determining a student's eligibility for financial aid, most colleges start with one or more formulas called methodologies. All colleges use the "Federal Methodology" to determine a student's eligibility for federal and state funds. Some private colleges also use an additional methodology, the "Institutional Methodology," to award their own dollars. Although the formulas are rigid and quite complex, the colleges have some leeway in how they use them. Students may find that different colleges offer the student different amounts of federal and state aid, based on how they apply the student's application data to the methodologies.

II. SCHOLARSHIP SAVVY

Start Early

During their senior year in high school, students are completing college applications. They are filling out financial aid applications. They may be enjoying the special aspects of the senior year in high school, while hopefully still succeeding at a challenging academic curriculum. These students will not want to spend time on a scholarship search or scholarship applications, many of which are due in the fall term of the senior year. Many scholarship applications include essays, projects, portfolios, or recommendations from others—which can be difficult to assemble at the last minute. Many parents, concerned that their seniors are already overstressed and overscheduled, don't encourage their seniors to focus on this potentially lucrative aspect of college applications. This is why it is crucial to start early.

Students and parents who start the scholarship searches early can identify potential scholarships in advance, at a time when they are more able to focus on the project. Students who start their searches as early as eighth and ninth grade have the student's entire high school career to develop the collateral material that scholarship donors want. Although there are no guarantees that scholarship donors will ask for the same projects and essays each year, they may. At the minimum, an early search for scholarships gives students a realistic idea of when the deadlines are and how much work is involved to secure funds from private donors.

For example, a tenth-grade student with an interest in biology may discover a scholarship for students like her, who conduct an original piece of biology research in high school and submit a research paper with their scholarship application. The future political science major may discover the scholarship requires an essay that happened to be covered in his junior year history class. Understanding in advance the work that scholarships require may allow students to integrate the work into their high school curriculum. Teachers will evaluate the work as it is produced, and students can rework it for the scholarship application. If the student needs a teacher letter of recommendation as part of the scholarship application, this can be arranged in advance without any surprises.

DON'T PANIC! WHAT IF MY CHILD IS ALREADY A SENIOR?

Late starters can still apply for and win scholarships, and some scholarships are offered not to incoming freshmen, but returning upperclassmen. After conducting the scholarship search, review the recommended scholarships and encourage your child to apply to the ones for which he is best qualified. Look for the scholarships that are likely to attract the fewest applications because they are limited to students who share your child's unique characteristics.

Incorporate College-Awarded Scholarships into College Selection

In an effort to fill classes with the best students, colleges offer a great deal of financial aid to students. In particular, many schools offer academic scholarships to those with noteworthy GPAs or test scores. When academically strong students attend, a college's average GPA and test scores creep higher, which over time improves the reputation of the institution.

Recruitment scholarships—often called presidential or dean's scholarships—are based on academic abilities or the student's interests. Information about these scholarships appears in each school's application paperwork and often in the school's view book, recruitment brochures, and admissions Web sites.

As you learned in chapter 3, as students identify Dream schools, Just Right schools, and No Problem schools, they should consider the scholarship opportunities available. If you choose a No Problem school that is likely to recruit a student like your child, then he is more likely to receive a generous merit-based scholarship. Your child's No Problem schools may recruit him with significant financial aid packages since they know that he is likely to be admitted to colleges with stronger reputations. Unless the No Problem school is significantly less expensive, they recognize that your student will often attend another college that is more selective.

Conversely, students should not expect to receive lucrative scholarship offers from their Dream schools. While all schools, including the country's most selective colleges, offer aid, not all schools use scholarships to recruit students. A Dream school for your child will look at his credentials and will know it is likely to be the most desirable education for the student. Thus, it is not as likely to offer a merit-based scholarship.

Rest assured, however, that scholarships exist for students even if they don't have a perfect GPA and SAT. When students consider their college selection, they should consider not only their objective academic position in the applicant pool, but also the following:

- Geography: Schools that attract most of their students from a localized area might be interested in recruiting students who come from outside that area. Regional private colleges that are interested in developing national application pools or reputations may invest some scholarship dollars in a student who lives outside of their geographic area.
- Course of Study: Schools may use scholarship dollars to attract students to academic programs that are traditionally undersubscribed or to one that the college is interested in building a strong program.
- Diversity: Schools may use scholarship dollars to attract students that are in some manner different from other students on campus. This may include gender, ethnicity, religion, political affiliation, et cetera.
- High School: Schools with a long-term focus may use scholarship dollars to attract students to campus from high schools with which the college hopes to build a relationship. The school's investment may pay off in a couple of ways. First, the student may return to the high school and "talk up" the college, creating interest where there was previously none. Second, if the student becomes a happy alumnus of the college, he may return to the high school as an alumni interviewer or recruiter, again building buzz for the college that did not already exist.

After the student identifies the colleges to which he is applying, he should review the college's admissions material to see what scholarship programs the colleges offer. Some colleges award scholarships to students based solely on the content of their admissions applications, such as the academic transcript, essays, and letters of recommendation. Other colleges may require supplemental material, such as an additional application for the scholarship; an additional letter of recommendation from a coach, a community service organization, or an employer; or an art portfolio.

Students may gear their admissions application not only with the intention of "getting in," but also to position themselves as good candidates for the school-specific scholarships. If the school offers specific scholarships for entrepreneurially minded business students, then the student might choose to write a college essay that illustrates entrepreneurial tendencies. If the school has scholarships for artistic students, then highlighting creative activities and artistic accomplishments might bring the student to the forefront for those dollars.

Look for Scholarships Outside of the Colleges

In addition to scholarships offered by colleges and universities, students can also seek funds from sources outside of the colleges, including professional organizations, local clubs, social clubs, research companies, and many others.

Before the Internet, identifying scholarships was difficult. Students would go to the library to review the scholarship books available. Some lucky students would have guidance counselors who had good records of possible scholarships. Students who put in the most legwork, and had the most luck, found and received the scholarships.

Today the search for scholarships has grown easier. Any scholarship donor that wants to provide funds for a student's college education can list themselves on free and centralized scholarship search databases, such as www.fastweb.com and www.college board.com, two sites I find to be quite comprehensive. Any student who matches the search criteria can find a scholarship simply by spending half an hour in front of a computer. The Internet has eliminated the luck factor from the scholarship search. It may also mean, however, that more candidates are applying for each scholarship, thereby decreasing the likelihood that any particular in-trepid, hardworking student will win them.

Because of the increased competition, students who start their searches earlier than their senior year in high school may have a leg up over students who don't plan ahead.

WARNING! YOU MUST ALERT COLLEGES ABOUT SCHOLARSHIP MONEY

If your child receives a scholarship from a source other than the colleges to which he is applying, he must report the award to each college from which he is seeking financial aid. Immediately upon notification, your child must write a cover letter to the director of financial aid at each school on his list and enclose a copy of the letter informing your child of the award.

Why? Scholarships, even those awarded as a reward for excellence, are a form of financial aid. Colleges must consider these awards as they allocate their own funds and federal and state funds. Students who fail to report these awards to the colleges are committing fraud.

On the positive side, sometimes a college will increase its own dollars when informed that a candidate has won other dollars. No matter the result, you simply must report scholarships to schools you are asking for aid.

III. FINANCIAL AID FORMS

As previously mentioned, the process of applying for financial aid involves various forms and different ways of getting information to the colleges. The financial aid process and the forms associated with it are not too difficult to understand. I will also highlight "simple facts" about these forms to make the process as painless as possible.

There are two major financial aid forms, and the colleges themselves may have their own forms as well.

- The FAFSA: Free Application for Federal Student Aid (required by almost all schools)
- The CSS: College Scholarship Service Profile (required by some schools)

You need to fill out only one of each form. Together, you and your student submit these forms to processors, indicating to which schools the students intends to apply. In turn, the FAFSA and CSS Profile information are electronically sent to the schools you have indicated. Each student therefore files the FAFSA and, if necessary, the CSS Profile, only once each year.

The Free Application for Federal Student Aid (FAFSA)

As a parent of a high school student, you have probably heard of the infamous FAFSA form. The FAFSA is the primary application for federal and state financial aid, as well as some private funding. Filing the FAFSA is a four-step process:

1. **answering the questions on the FAFSA;**
2. **selecting colleges that will receive the FAFSA data;**
3. **signing the FAFSA;**
4. **reviewing the Student Aid Report (SAR).**

1. Answering the questions on the FAFSA

The FAFSA form can be filed in one of two ways: online or on paper. The electronic FAFSA can be found online at www.fafsa.ed.gov, while the paper version can be obtained from your child's guidance office or from any college financial aid office. There is no fee for filing the FAFSA, so if you are asked to pay to file the FAFSA, make sure that you are using the correct form or the correct Web site.

When it comes to deadlines, the earliest you can submit your FAFSA form for processing is January 1 of the year in which the academic year begins. For example, the FAFSA for the academic year of August 15 to June 1 becomes available on January 1 *prior* to the school year (and not in the middle of it). Be careful to file the FAFSA for the correct academic year; during most of the year, two different FAFSAs are available.

The FAFSA asks biographical questions about the student and financial questions about the student and parent(s). The income questions are based on the student and parent income tax returns for the prior calendar year. The college-set deadlines for filing the FAFSA are typically earlier than April 15, despite the fact that many people have not completed their income tax returns. Therefore, students and parents are permitted to use estimated income figures when completing the FAFSA. A comprehensive, question-by-question instruction manual for filing the FAFSA is available from the United States Department of Education at http://student aid.ed.gov/students/publications/completing_fafsa/index.html.

2. Selecting colleges that will receive the FAFSA data

After completing the FAFSA questions, you will need to indicate which colleges will receive the FAFSA data. Each college has a six-digit Federal School Code. If the student files the paper version of the FAFSA, he can obtain each college's Federal School Code from the college's financial aid office. Students who file the online FAFSA will be able to get the Federal School Codes online, as part of the FAFSA application Web site.

3. Signing the FAFSA

Next, students must "sign" their FAFSA, certifying that all information provided on the form is accurate. For most undergraduate students who are younger than twenty-four years old, one parent must also sign the FASFA. Space for signatures is provided on the paper version of the FAFSA. Students who file the FAFSA electronically, and their parent, can "sign" the FAFSA by typing their federal PIN numbers into the online application, when asked. The student will have her own four-digit PIN, and the student will have a *different* four-digit PIN. PINs can be obtain

Web site www.pin.ed.gov at any time. The student and the student's parent should apply for PINs at least a week before filing the FAFSA. PINs can be used not only to "sign" the FAFSA, but also to sign federal student and parent loan promissory notes.

4. Reviewing the Student Aid Report (SAR)

After the student submits the FAFSA, the Department of Education will process the application and send the student a Student Aid Report (SAR). The SAR will consist of a list of all the answers to the FAFSA questions, a comments section describing problems and follow-up steps for the student, and perhaps an Expected Family Contribution (EFC).

It is important that the student and the family review the SAR to verify that all the answers are correct. This is especially important for people who submit a paper FAFSA: the federal processor scans these forms and some numbers may register incorrectly. The SAR can be used to correct errors and update any estimated income and tax figures submitted on the FAFSA. The SAR can be reviewed and updated online if the student filed the FAFSA electronically, or on paper, if it was filed manually. If the SAR is used to update data, it must be signed. The same PINs used to sign the FAFSA can be used to sign the revised SAR.

DON'T PANIC! WHAT IF I MAKE A MISTAKE FILLING OUT THE FORMS?

The Comments section on the SAR will alert you to any problems that the department found when processing the original application. Each comment will include steps to resolve the problem, if possible. For example, if the Department of Education is unable to make an exact match between the student's name, Social Security number, and birthday on the FAFSA and Social Security Administration records, the student will be instructed to send the college a copy of his Social Security card.

Most of the time, these problems can be easily resolved if the student follows the directions and submits the proper documentation to colleges. As long as the student is a United States citizen or permanent resident, most issues can be resolved. The college's financial aid office can be a good resource if you have questions about how to resolve an issue.

If there are no problems to be resolved (and sometimes even if there are), the SAR will include the student's Expected Family Contribution (EFC). The EFC is the end result of the federal financial aid formula. Colleges use the EFC to allocate federal financial aid. This may be the first time the student sees a number suggesting how much college will cost.

It is critical to remember that the EFC does not necessarily represent the actual amount the student and their family will pay for college. Colleges allocate federal and state funds based on the SAR EFC, but may use other formulas or methods to allocate other kinds of funds.

The College Scholarship Service Profile (CSS Profile)

To allocate their own financial aid funds, private colleges sometimes use a formula that differs from the federal formula. They may require financial aid applicants to complete their own institutional application or the CSS Profile form.

Note that Profile is *not* a free service; there are fees associated with this application. Filing the CSS Profile form is a two-step process:

1. registration
2. application.

1. Registration

You must first register with the CSS Profile service before the student can obtain the CSS Profile application. Registration is available for a small fee online at www.collegeboard.com. It is important to note: as part of the CSS Profile registration process, you are asked to list schools that your student is applying to. *However, you need to list only the colleges or universities that require the*

CSS Profile. You do not need to list any schools that need only the FAFSA form. The Profile costs $18 per college, or program, to which the student wants the application sent.

2. Application

After the student registers with Profile, CSS will provide him with a customized application that contains basic questions required by all colleges, and supplemental questions required by the specific colleges to which the student is applying. You and your child will complete and submit the Profile application to CSS. CSS, in turn, sends the application data to each college the student indicated on their registration form.

Here are some additional tips when filing the Profile:

- Do not include a school or program at the registration step unless that school requires the CSS Profile. Many colleges do not require a Profile. Also, some colleges only require the Profile from first-time applicants; ask the financial aid office to make filing in the future easier.
- Every school that requires the CSS Profile also requires the FAFSA. Even though the Profile includes all the questions that are on the FAFSA, private colleges must have a valid FAFSA on file before they can process federal and state financial aid for the student.

Filling out the CSS and FAFSA forms are a large part of the financial aid application process. However, they are not the only piece of the process that can ultimately determine the financial package you receive.

IV. UNUSUAL CIRCUMSTANCES

It is beneficial to be thorough while filling out the FAFSA and CSS forms, but as you file financial aid applications, you may realize that the forms often prevent you from telling schools your whole story. There are steps you can take to ensure your entire situation is considered. You may need to contact financial aid offices directly if there are unusual circumstances in your family finances. If you look carefully, you will even see that, on the first page, the FAFSA tells you to do just this: "If you or your family has unusual circumstances (such as loss of employment), complete and submit this form as instructed and then consult with the financial aid office at the college you plan to attend." I strongly urge you to take the FAFSA up on this suggestion; you want to do everything you can to qualify for aid.

If necessary, you should send an "unusual circumstances" letter to the financial aid offices of all colleges to which your child is applying. It is perfectly acceptable to address the letter to the Director of Financial Aid, but you may personalize the letter, as well. A complete "unusual circumstances" letter needs to include the following information:

- Your child's full name and birthday. If your child already attends college, or the undergraduate admissions office issued your child a student ID number with their application, include this information as well.
- A brief explanation of the unusual circumstance.
- Dollar values that specifically describe how the circumstance "affects your need for financial aid."
- Documentation, if possible, that shows that you are actually spending the aforementioned dollars.

Note that an "unusual circumstances" letter that is submitted after a financial aid offer has been made is called an "appeal." Write this letter as soon as you can. If you know about the circumstance before you file the financial aid application, mail it to the financial aid office about the same time you file the FAFSA. The individual colleges will ensure it is matched with the student's financial aid application.

If the unusual circumstance occurs after the financial aid application is filed, or even after you receive a financial aid award or during your child's enrollment in college, call the college and ask if they have an "appeal form." You will write the same letter, but the school may have a specific procedure they would like you to follow.

After you get a financial aid offer, call the school and ask if the unusual circumstance was considered as they prepared your financial aid package. If it was not, find out if it can be reconsidered, or if the school would like additional information from you that might make them reconsider their denial of sufficient funds.

Unusual circumstances are often challenging to identify or explain. Here are a few specific and most common instances that could grant additional consideration from a financial aid office.

1. The income reported on the FAFSA is unusually high

The financial aid applications for each academic year are based on the previous tax year. If your previous year's income was unusually high for any reason, you will want to let the school know. Incomes can be unusually high for many reasons including:

- a self-employed person had a very successful year;
- an employee received a bonus that will not be granted again;
- the taxpayer sold stocks, mutual funds, or property and realized a capital gain;
- the taxpayer won the lottery or a prize;
- the taxpayer exercised stock options;
- the taxpayer cashed out an IRA or pension plan;
- the taxpayer converted a traditional IRA into a Roth IRA;
- the taxpayer cashed in U.S. Savings Bonds and reported all the accumulated interest in one year.

When reporting this type of unusual circumstance, make sure the college knows specifically *how much* of the income on the tax return is "unusual." Document the one-time nature of the income by sending a copy of tax returns from earlier years that prove and reinforce the absence of the income, along with any other documents that show that the income will not reappear in the upcoming year.

2. A parent loses a job

On the opposite end of the spectrum, just as irregular surplus income should be identified, so should a noticeable deficit. If one of the student's parents' incomes will be lower in the forthcoming academic year than in the prior calendar one, send a letter to the school that describes the change. Include the last date of employment, a description of the severance package, if any, and an estimate of how difficult it will be for the parent to find a new job. Include a copy of the termination letter as documentation.

3. A parent retires

Often, especially for the youngest child in a family, a parent will retire prior to or during the college application process. If this is the case, in your letter let the school know the last date of employment, the date retirement benefits (including Social Security) begin, and a description of these benefits. Include letters from the employer and pension plans that support the numbers. If the retiring parent is young, the letter should include an explanation that lets the school know why the parent is leaving employment at an early age.

4. The family has higher than usual nonreimbursed medical costs

When a parent or sibling incurs atypical medical costs, this is another instance where a letter of unusual circumstances is applicable. Describe the medical conditions that you are paying for, how much you are paying, and how frequently. Include a copy of your tax return 1040 Schedule A, if you have one, as well as receipts or bills from the medical provider. If you have a letter from the insurance company that explains their refusal to pay for the services, include a copy of that, too.

5. The parents are repaying their own educational debts

These days, more and more people are going back to school. If you are still repaying student loans from your own undergraduate education, or from any graduate programs, let the school know both the outstanding principal balance on the loans and the required monthly payment. Include a copy of a payment coupon or end-of-year statement with the letter.

6. The parents support their own parents

If you are paying for care for the student's grandparents or other family members, or sending money to relatives to support them, let the school know how much you are paying on a monthly or annual basis. Include copies of checks that demonstrate the regularity of the payments and an explanation of the reason you are making them.

7. The parents are repaying parent loans for children older than the current student

For families with several children, it's common for parents to pay for more than one college education at once. In this letter, let the colleges know the number of children you have already put through college. Also include the principal balance of any outstanding parent loans and the required monthly payments for each. Enclose copies of end-of-year statements and payment coupons with the letter.

8. The parents are paying for private precollege education for a younger sibling

Frequently, a student applicant has younger siblings with outstanding education bills. For example, if you are paying for a younger child's private education, this is another expense colleges should consider when determining your financial aid. Inform the college of how much you are paying and why you have chosen private education over public education. With the letter, include a copy of the first bill of the year that depicts the yearly school tuition.

9. The family is recovering from an act of nature

If your family has suffered from a fire, flood, earthquake, tornado, or other disaster that destroyed property, describe the following:

- the nature of the disaster;
- the date the disaster happened;

- the property destroyed;
- the value of the property destroyed;
- the value of any insurance payments made as a result of the disaster;
- the amount the family had to pay out of pocket to recover from the damage;
- the amount of wages lost as a result of the disaster.

For substantial damage, most families cannot afford the large unforeseen costs. So, if you borrowed money to cover the costs of the recovery and are still making payments on the recovery loan, include information about the size of the outstanding loan and the required monthly payment.

10. Other circumstances

This is not an exhaustive list. If there are any other circumstances that you want the colleges to know about, any regular payments or large lump-sum payments, include them in your letter. Remember to include dollar values, dates, and specific descriptions, and be prepared to send documentation that shows that you actually incurred the expenses (or will have to incur the expenses).

V. NEGOTIATING: THE FIRST FINANCIAL AID AWARD DOESN'T HAVE TO BE THE LAST

When assessing financial aid awards, most students and their families accept each award at face value. They accept or reject offers of admission after comparing the financial aid awards and determining which college offers the most value to the student. Many colleges, however, are receptive to requests to rereview the financial aid award. As you just learned, families can bring unusual circumstances to the attention of colleges as part of a need-based financial aid application, so that the college has a better picture of the family's ability to pay for college. Similarly, a request can be made as part of a negotiation process designed to secure more recruitment scholarship dollars from the college.

NEW RULE OF COLLEGE ADMISSIONS: TAKE ADVANTAGE OF THE COMPETITIVE COLLEGE ENVIRONMENT

Even the most competitive colleges will take a second look at a financial aid award if a competitive school offers a significantly different level of aid (although, do note that some colleges do not negotiate). They may be simply looking for mistakes that they or the more generous college made as part of a need-based financial aid analysis. Or they may be looking for a reason to provide the student with additional funds.

Colleges that are aggressively competing to fill their seats with increasingly stronger classes of students and those that are locked in intense competition with "rival" schools may be interested in supplementing an early financial aid award with additional funds if a rival school has offered a better, or even simply a comparable, financial aid offer. Some schools even hold back some financial aid so that they are able to respond affirmatively to *any* request for additional help.

At the minimum, students should contact the financial aid office at each college they would like to attend and let them know that one (or more) of the other colleges has offered a better financial aid package. Include a copy of the better award or awards with the letter, so that the targeted colleges know the student has a less expensive educational choice. Don't be too surprise if Just Right schools don't match the awards of No Problem schools, or Dream schools don't match the awards of Just Right schools. But, in general, the colleges won't even consider offering additional funds if you don't ask. The worst that will happen is the colleges will decline to increase their financial aid offer.

VI. THE FINANCIAL AID STATEMENT (FAS)

The answer to a financial aid application will be a college's Financial Aid Statement (FAS). The FAS lists the specific financial aid awards that the school, the government, and other sources will make available to the student in the relevant academic year. The FAS may look something like this:

This Financial Aid Statement is for the current Academic Year only. We assume that you will live in an on-campus dormitory and attend classes full-time during the fall and spring terms. If either of these assumptions is incorrect, notify the Student Financial Aid Office immediately.

Cost of Attendance:	$15,650	Total Financial Aid:	$9,800
Estimated:			
Tuition	$5,100		
Mandatory Fees	$200	Dean's Scholarship	$4,000
Room	$3,750	Federal Stafford Loan	$3,500
Board	$3,000	Federal Work/Study	$1,500
Books	$900	Pell Grant	$800
Personal Expenses	$1,600		
Travel	$1,000		
Loan Fees	$100		

This financial aid offer is subject to change should the Student Financial Aid Office receive new information from or about you.

Notify the Student Financial Aid Office immediately if you receive any scholarships from sources outside of the college or will be paying for part of your education with a prepaid tuition plan contract.

The FAS figures for Estimated Costs and Specific Awards usually cover an entire academic year, unlike student bills, which list semester costs. With that in mind, understand that the FAS is not a bill. The dollar values listed on the FAS, for tuition and other parts of the cost of attendance, are merely estimates used to calculate financial aid awards. Ultimately, your child's education may cost more or less than the figures on the FAS.

WARNING! READ THE FAS SUPPORTING MATERIALS CAREFULLY

Be aware that the FAS does not reflect any choices that the student will make about housing, meals plans, health insurance, or any other aspects of his or her college experience.

Plus, the individual awards your child receives may have restrictions. Be sure to read the supporting materials carefully before assuming that all awards are appropriate or available. You may need to take additional steps to secure the funds listed on the FAS. For example, the student will have to sign a promissory note and experience "loan entrance counseling" before he or she is allowed to receive student loan funds.

VII. THE STUDENT BILL

In late spring or early summer, after your child decides which school to attend, the college will send your child the first college bill. As a parent, you should help your child understand this bill, the various charges, and what everything means. Unlike the financial aid statement, the bill will reflect actual costs your child will incur. These fees may be different from those on the FAS and will be based on choices regarding meal plans, housing options, health insurance, or other miscellaneous decisions.

Assuming there have been no changes to the financial aid statement example, your child's first bill may look something like this:

Total Current Charges	$5,855
Tuition	$2,550
Athletic Club Fee	$35
Student Fee	$100
Double Room in Random Hall	$1,800
Key Deposit	$20
Meal Plan: 14 meals per week	$1,350

Anticipated Credits:	$4,097.50
Dean's Scholarship	$2,000
Federal Stafford Loan	$1,697.50
Pell Grant	$400
Credits:	$200
Admissions Deposit	$200
Balance Due:	$1,557.50

The student bill reflects actual charges for the upcoming term, *not the entire academic year*, like the FAS reported. I highly recommend reading all of the directions and instructions on the financial information. If you and your child follow the college's instructions about securing the funds, often the college will reduce the amount the student needs to pay, even if the college has yet to receive any funds. In addition, any work-related financial aid awards are never reflected on the bill.

The financial aid process is lengthy and can be quite stressful, but if there is one consolation, perhaps it is this: even though you'll have to apply for financial aid each year your child is in college, experience is a great teacher. You'll have a much easier time with this process next year!

CONCLUSION: WHAT NEXT?

A Q&A with Lloyd Peterson, Vice President of Education, College Coach, and Former Senior Admissions Officer, Yale University

Congratulations on finishing the college application process with your child! As a senior member of College Coach's team of counselors, I am pleased to say that we have an excellent record of helping students develop the very best applications they can, resulting in admission to their desired schools. If you have followed the expert advice provided by my colleagues in this book, I believe you will have guided your child, calmly and strategically, to find and get accepted to a school he feels excited to attend.

After reviewing the ten comprehensive chapters (including chapter 9, which I wrote), I felt we needed to address a few additional topics that are top-of-mind with parents once their children's applications have been submitted and the results start coming in. Here is a list of the most frequently asked questions regarding the postapplication process.

My answers are based on my work as vice president of education at College Coach, as well as two decades working in senior admissions positions on college campuses, including Yale University, Vassar College, and Colorado College. I have always been personally and professionally invested in making certain that students have a smooth transition from their homes to the college campus environment. I am pleased to do the same for your family.

Q: How do I help my child choose a school after the decisions have come in?

A: Ideally, if your child has completed the process recommended in this book and his academic and extracurricular interests are clearly prioritized, the final decision should not be difficult to make. However, some students do face dilemmas in making a choice.

First, I suggest you forget about the schools' brand names. Revisit, for a moment, what is most important. Ask your child to give serious thought to what he wants to study. Is he comfortable with what each school offers in his most favorite subject areas? Does your child plan to study abroad? Will lab or studio work be a factor? Is your child comfortable with each school's faculty advising system—their level of involvement and accessibility?

Next, your teen must be honest about which schools meet his cultural, social, spiritual, athletic, and artistic needs. At this point in the process, students must again ask themselves what they would enjoy doing on a Friday evening or Saturday afternoon. Remind your child to keep the answers as close to the heart as possible. If your daughter would rather hang out with friends instead of going to a museum or art gallery, then she needs to acknowledge that when making her final choice.

Finally, do not hesitate to get more information about the schools your child is considering. I suggest you talk to currently enrolled students and recent graduates, because I have found them to be the most candid about their colleges. To do this, contact the admissions office and ask if they would provide a list of currently enrolled students from your hometown or surrounding area, and/or a similar list of recent graduates. Admissions offices should have these lists readily available. Encourage your undecided child to give these people a call rather than e-mailing them. Recommend to your teen that he listen for the excitement in their voices, or lack thereof, about dorm life, classes, campus life, student activities, and whatever else might help him make the final decision.

Q: What strategies do you recommend if my child is placed on a wait list?

A: If your child is wait listed, the number-one decision he has to make is whether he really wants to attend that school. At this point, he probably will have multiple acceptances and rejections. Look closely at where the wait list school falls on your child's list. Feel free to drop it if he doesn't really want to attend. Colleges will provide accepted students with a simple form or card to fill out to state their intention to attend the school or not, so turning down an offer is quick and easy. (Of course, if a child neglects to send back the form, the school will assume he is not planning to attend.)

If the school is a contender, then I'll first offer a few words about wait list activity. Students are placed on the wait list because the admissions office simply ran out of room in the freshman class to admit them. The combination of academics and extracurricular activities drew strong interest from the admissions committee, but in the final cut the student wasn't quite strong enough to admit, but was too strong to reject.

Accordingly, wait lists are rarely ranked from an academic perspective. If the admissions committee were not interested in your child academically, he would have been rejected in the first place. So grades and test scores are not a factor in getting your child off of the wait list.

Rather, students are taken from the wait list because they meet some other need in which admissions is interested. For instance, there may be no one thus far in the freshman class from Alaska, and the school has a student on the wait list from Anchorage who is willing to come. Or students are admitted from the wait list because the complexion of their candidacy changed for the better since the application deadline, and they have all but committed to attending the college if chosen from the wait list.

If your child is wait listed and does want to attend the school in question, be sure to fill out the school's wait list form and send it back immediately. Second, I recommend that your child write an additional letter to the admissions committee saying that if the school accepts him off of the wait list, he will definitely attend. In the letter, he should highlight something specific that might make him a better applicant than when he originally submitted an application. In one case, a young woman was able to share with the committee that she had recently won a national playwriting prize, and she submitted her play and a newspaper clipping about the award. As a result, New York University accepted her from its wait list.

In the meantime, if you accept another school while you are waiting, you have to be willing to lose your deposit.

Q: Can we appeal a rejection?
A: You can appeal, but it's generally a waste of time. In my twenty-five years of experience, I don't recall seeing a successful appeal of a rejection.

Q: What if my child isn't accepted anywhere?
A: If you have followed the advice in this book and made sure your child has applied to a careful mix of Dreams, Just Rights, and No Problems, this should not be an issue. If you do face this result, I advise you consider the following options:

1. You have to reflect on what went wrong. To my knowledge, at College Coach we've never worked with a student who hasn't been accepted anywhere. Really think about why your child was not accepted anywhere. Were you looking at his transcript through rose-colored glasses? Does your child have a personal problem that might have been reflected in his letters of recommendation? The most likely scenario is that you did not realistically assess your child's academic and extracurricular credentials and therefore you applied too aggressively.

2. Decide what your child wants to do next. These days it is not uncommon to start college a year late. Many students choose to take a year off to work or travel. Some have no other choice due to military or religious commitments. Regardless of the reason, admissions officers can look very

favorably on an applicant who has taken a year off and done something fruitful.

During the year off, students may want to consider a career-related internship, a study abroad program, or an extra year at a private school. Many private boarding and day schools offer a "postgraduate year" that allows students to embellish their academic or extracurricular profiles. Sometimes parents send their child to postgraduate programs because they began school a year early, or perhaps they skipped a grade along the way, and the extra year is for personal developmental reasons.

No matter what a student chooses to do in the year off, he must add something new to his application if he plans to reapply to colleges the following year, and especially if he plans to reapply to the same schools. Bagging groceries at the supermarket and working out are not enough. My best recommendation for a productive year before reapplying is for your child to take a class and get an A, plus work at an internship related to his career interests while also volunteering in a way that is related to that internship or his application theme.

If your child does decide to take a class, consider courses at a school with open enrollment, such as a community college. Even more than high school grades and test scores, colleges are impressed by people who excel at other colleges, despite the level of rigor. College-level work is college-level work. Your teen can begin to rebuild his grade point average as well as his confidence. Extracurricular involvement will help with next year's admissions process and could also sharpen vocational interests and his application theme. This approach adds to the application file, ensuring that the admissions committee is not reviewing the same set of documents that resulted in bad news before.

3. A final strategy involves looking for colleges late in April and May that still have room in their freshman class to admit students. For a variety of legitimate reasons, there are

colleges and universities still looking to fill spots long after the May 1 reply date and oftentimes into June. These are not open-enrollment institutions, but the later in the summer it gets, the more willing these colleges are to consider late applicants who do not have A-average transcripts.

This list of colleges is developed and maintained by the National Association of College Admissions Counseling (NACAC), the group which governs all U.S. admissions and college counseling activity, and can be found at www.NACAC.com.

Q: Does the end of senior year really matter to colleges?

A: The final two semesters of high school do count in the minds of colleges. Although admissions officers will have made a decision on your child's application long before he graduates, a consistent academic performance is expected, and this expectation is usually mentioned in your child's acceptance letter.

At some schools, severe grade slippage can result in a college's rescinding its admissions offer. Although I find that harsh, colleges take this very seriously and your child cannot begin to slack off, especially during the spring of senior year when this dynamic is most dangerous. Most seniors find concentrating on school extremely difficult from March to June. The weather is getting nicer, spring break has come and gone, and the admissions cycle is winding down. "AP," for some, no longer means advanced placement, but "auto pilot," as they begin to cruise toward the diploma! When I was an admissions officer, I had no interest in pulling students out of the class over grade slippage, but I did require a written explanation from the student, not the parent, if serious slippage did occur.

Q: After being accepted, should my child visit campuses, attend open houses, and/or go to accepted student receptions?

A: Any events for accepted students are nice to attend, because for the first time students are not trying to make an impression on the school; the school is trying to make an impression on them.

Admitted students walk on campuses in April in a different mind-set. At this point, the school wants admitted students to attend, so the student is in the driver's seat. It shows. There seems to be a swagger in their walk at open houses and receptions.

These types of gatherings also provide a great chance for students to meet potential classmates and roommates, ask questions, and begin to get involved immediately in campus life. And they can be fun!

Q: What happens if my child wants to transfer? Do the same "rules" apply to transfer applications, or is it a different process?

A: The transfer admissions decision is driven by the work students have done while in college. They are college students now, and the high school record, though requested, is usually secondary. The more college your child has, the more important the college transcript will be. Of course, if your child attempts to transfer after only one semester of college, he will essentially be considered like a high school student because he has very little college experience. However, if he transfers after one or two full years of college, his college grades and activities will be more important, and his high school credentials won't matter as much.

In general, transfer admissions are much harder to predict because there are different variables to consider. The number of transfer students a college can take is usually dictated by the number of freshmen enrolling, the number of currently enrolled students studying abroad or on leave of absence, and housing availability, as well as financial aid options. Subsequently, a top student at Harvard could be rejected as a transfer applicant to Boston University if BU simply has no spots available.

The number of open slots available at a college is definitely an issue when transferring. I suggest, however, before your child begins poring over enrollment stats, to step back and consider the following. Admissions offices that accept transfer students (and not all do) welcome them for the same reasons first-year students are sought after. They bring an intellectual curiosity and extracurricular energy to the community. Transfer students can often add something extra. They are usually a bit older and presumably more mature and focused, which is very appealing to admissions committees. In a similar vein, admissions officers are interested in transfer students bringing with them a different college perspective based on what they have already experienced. The more different the perspective—different type of school, geographic location, et cetera—the more interested admissions may be in the applicant.

That's the other reason a top Harvard student might not be accepted as a transfer to Boston University. Such an applicant would be applying from one large urban campus to another large urban campus. Will the Friday night conversation be that much different? A student from Cal State Northridge or Colorado College may have better luck because his past college experience would have been so different.

Q: What happens if none of the financial aid awards are enough to allow your child to attend college?

A: In an ideal world, planning will prevent this worst-case scenario from ever happening. As you have read earlier in this book, families for whom the expense of college will be a major factor should consider cost in their child's list of Dreams, Just Rights, and No Problems. This refers back to the "financial safety school" issue discussed in chapters 3 and 10.

If you do find yourself in this situation, contacting the admissions office is the necessary first step. Ask to speak with the admissions officer responsible for your child's application. Then explain that you are working with the financial aid office. If you cannot respond to the offer of admission by May 1 because of financial aid issues, you do not want the admissions office to give your child's spot in the class away. If you miss the May 1 deadline, losing your place in the class is a sure possibility, so communicate first with the admissions office.

Contacting the financial aid office is the next step. Most admissions decisions are final. There is no appeal or negotiation process. Financial aid offices, on the other hand, may not negotiate but will often agree to review your file again if you can present new information. For example, if you never mentioned earlier that unexpected dental fees will have a major impact on the monthly budget during your son's freshman year in college, that fact may trigger an adjustment in your family's favor. Or, you may have a situation where your son has received offers from Colleges A and B. College B's financial award is a bit stronger, but your son wants to attend College A. Feel free to share College B's award with College A. This is another good example of how new information could trigger an adjustment in your favor.

You also can continue to search for scholarship dollars that have not been used to this point, although this effort should come last. By April in any given year most scholarship money has been distributed, but scholarship deadlines do run all year round and students can apply for scholarships during every year of college. It's certainly worth a cursory look.

Acknowledgments

We would like to thank a few of the many people whose efforts have made this book a reality and College Coach a success:

The contributors to this book, namely Heather Beveridge, Karen Crowley, Jennifer Duran, Nicole Eichin, Brooke Stengel Fitzgerald, Scott Ham, Julia Jones, Karen Spencer, Robert Weinerman, and, in particular, Lloyd Peterson for lending expertise to this project and so many others.

Tracy Beard, Melissa Jacoby, Ryan Leer, Christopher Morton, and the rest of College Coach's employees, for their continued effort and ongoing support.

Carla Glasser, Shannon Crane, Lindsey Pollack, and Annie Ronan for their assistance throughout the writing and editing process.

Axel Freudman and Peggy Jaeger from AIG for sharing their innovative spirit and helping us change the way that corporations think about education.

Finally we would like to thank the thousands of families that have trusted us to successfully guide them through the college admissions process.

Contact Information

Phone: 1.877.40.COACH

E-mail: info@getintocollege.com, mailto:info@getintocollege.com

Web site: www.getintocollege.com

Mail:

College Coach

233 Needham Street, Suite 200

Newton, MA 02464

Index